Inside Your Brain

Brain Works

Inside Your Brain

Eric H. Chudler, Ph.D.

CHELSEA HOUSE
PUBLISHERS
An imprint of Infobase Publishing

*Thanks go to Sandy, Kelly, and Sam who have heard about
this "brain stuff" for many years and to my parents, Sunny and Al,
who taught me that the only way to find the answer is to ask the question.*

Inside Your Brain

Copyright © 2007 by Infobase Publishing

Chelsea House
An imprint of Infobase Publishing
132 West 31st Street
New York NY 10001

Library of Congress Cataloging-in-Publication Data

Chudler, Eric H.
    Inside your brain / Eric H. Chudler.
      p. cm. — (Brain works)
    Includes bibliographical references and index.
    ISBN 0-7910-8944-4 (hardcover)
    1. Brain—Juvenile literature.   2. Neurophysiology—Juvenile literature. I. Title.
  II. Series
    QP376.C494 2006
    612.8'2—dc22   2006020927

Text design by Keith Trego
Cover design by Takeshi Takahashi

Printed in the United States of America

Bang KT 10 9 8 7 6 5 4 3 2 1

This book is printed on acid-free paper.

All links and Web addresses were checked and verified to be correct at the time of publication. Because of the dynamic nature of the Web, some addresses and links may have changed since publication and may no longer be valid.

Table of Contents

Introduction

Prepare yourself for a journey to a world filled with sights, sounds, tastes, and smells. You will not need a suitcase or ticket for your travels, but you should be prepared for unexpected adventures. Your journey will take you to the world inside your brain.

There are many good reasons to learn about the brain. The brain controls all of your thoughts, emotions, and actions. The wonder of this fantastic three-pound organ should fascinate us all. There are also practical reasons to study the brain. Damage to the brain may cause severe problems such as the inability to move, talk, and feel. Someone you know may have a brain disorder such as epilepsy, depression, cerebral palsy, Parkinson's disease, or Alzheimer's disease. The people (and their friends and relatives) affected by these disorders pay a high physical, emotional, and financial price.

We must understand how the brain works so we can develop new treatments and cures for these disorders.

This book is for anyone interested in learning about the brain and nervous system. Each chapter starts with background information to give you an overview of the chapter topic. The background information is followed by experiments, games, and demonstrations to help you understand these new ideas. This book is not a textbook. Rather, the book is organized to supplement other material to help you learn about the nervous system.

The activities, projects, and experiments in this book will make you think and ask questions about how your brain works. Asking questions is good—remember that the only bad questions are those that you do not ask.

The brain is a world
consisting of a number of unexplored
continents and great stretches of unknown territory.
—Neuroanatomist Santiago Ramón y Cajal (1843–1926)

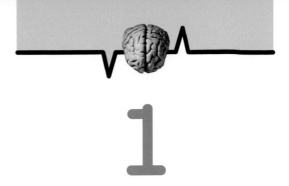

1

Brain Basics

The human brain is three pounds of the most complex matter known to man. Your brain is responsible for everything you have done in the past, everything that you are doing right now, and everything that you will do in the future. Reading, writing, remembering, crying, laughing, running, talking—all are examples of your brain at work. Your brain also receives information from the outside world and from inside your body. Your brain must understand this information and send signals to muscles, organs, and glands to control what your body does.

The human body is made up of trillions of cells. Cells in the nervous system act as your body's communication system, sending information from place to place to coordinate your body's actions. The nervous system has two main types of cells: nerve

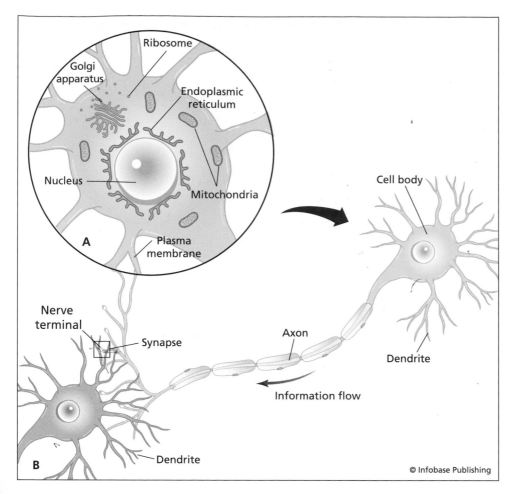

Figure 1.1 **(A) Neurons, like all cells, contain specialized components known as organelles. (B) Electrical signals travel down the axon of a neuron toward the dendrite of an adjacent neuron. The junction between the two neurons is called a synapse.**

cells (**neurons**) and glial cells (**glia**). Neurons carry messages to other neurons, muscles, organs, or glands. The human brain has approximately 100 billion neurons. Glial cells help support the brain and bring nutrients to neurons.

The brain has at least ten times more glial cells than nerve cells.

NEURONS

Neurons are similar to other cells of the body because they are surrounded by a cell membrane, make proteins, produce energy, and contain genes. Neurons are different from other cells of the body because they have specialized branches called **dendrites** and **axons** (Figure 1.1). Dendrites bring information to the cell body and axons take information away from the cell body. A neuron can have many dendrites, but only one axon. Also, unlike other cells of the body,

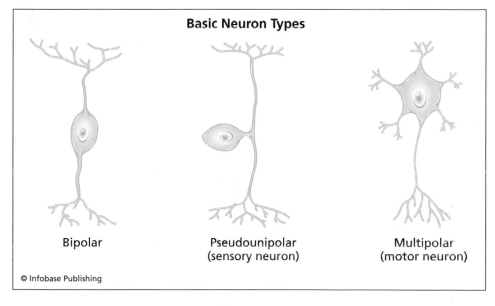

Basic Neuron Types

Bipolar

Pseudounipolar
(sensory neuron)

Multipolar
(motor neuron)

© Infobase Publishing

Figure 1.2 **Neurons are classified by their structure. The illustration above shows three different types of neurons. Each type of neuron has a different role within the nervous system.**

neurons communicate with each other using electrical and chemical signals.

Neurons have a variety of shapes and sizes (Figure 1.2). Some neurons are very short (less than a millimeter in length) and some neurons are very long (3 feet [1 meter] or more). For example, the axon of a neuron stretching from the spinal cord to a muscle in the foot can be more than 3 feet in length.

HOW DO NEURONS SEND MESSAGES?

Signals move from neuron to neuron across a small space within a **synapse**, the junction between two neurons. Although most synapses occur between an axon and a dendrite, they can also be located between an axon and another axon or between an axon and a cell body.

Neurons are like small batteries because they can produce electricity. For communication between neurons to occur, an electrical signal must travel down the axon of a neuron to the **synaptic terminal**. This electrical signal is called an **action potential**. The size of the action potential within a neuron is always the same. Also, a neuron either sends a full action potential or it does not send one at all. This is called the "all or none" principle of neurotransmission.

When an action potential reaches the synaptic terminal, it triggers the release of chemicals. These chemicals, called **neurotransmitters**, move across the synapse and attach to special places (**receptors**) on another neuron. When a neurotransmitter attaches to a receptor, it makes the receiving neuron either more or less likely to fire its own action potential. Receptors for different neurotransmitters have different shapes. Only neurotransmitters that fit the shape of the receptor will have an effect. This action is similar to a lock and key: the key (the neurotransmitter) must fit the lock (the receptor). There are more than 50 different neurotransmitters in the brain. Common neurotransmitters are acetylcholine, dopamine, serotonin, glutamate, gamma-aminobutyric acid (GABA), and norepinephrine.

Inside a Neuron

A neuron contains many of the same organelles as other cells in the body, including the following:

◆ Nucleus – Contains genetic material (chromosomes) that includes information for cell development and the synthesis of proteins necessary for cell maintenance and survival. Covered by a membrane.

◆ Nucleolus – Produces ribosomes necessary for translation of genetic information into proteins.

◆ Nissl bodies – Groups of ribosomes used for protein synthesis.

◆ Endoplasmic reticulum (ER) – System of tubes that transport materials within the cytoplasm; can have ribosomes (rough ER) or no ribosomes (smooth ER). Rough ER is important for protein synthesis.

◆ Golgi apparatus – Membrane-bound structure important for packaging peptides and proteins (including neurotransmitters) into vesicles.

◆ Microtubules/Neurofilaments – Structures that transport materials within a neuron and may be used for structural support.

◆ Mitochondria – Produce energy to fuel cellular activities.

The action of a neurotransmitter can be stopped four different ways:

1 Diffusion: the neurotransmitter drifts away from its target and can no longer act on a receptor.
2 Enzymatic degradation (deactivation): an enzyme changes the structure of the neurotransmitter so it is not recognized by the receptor.
3 **Astrocytes**, one type of glial cell, remove neurotransmitters from the synapse.
4 Reuptake: the neurotransmitter molecule is taken back into the axon terminal that released it.

GLIA

Although there are approximately 100 billion neurons in the brain, there are at least 10 times that many glial cells in the brain. Glial cells do not send nerve impulses (action potentials), but they do have many important functions. In fact, without glia, neurons would not work properly. Glial cells provide physical and nutritional support for neurons, clean up dead brain cells, and provide the insulation for neurons. These cells may also influence the way neurons communicate with each other.

Glial cells are different than nerve cells in several ways:

◆ Neurons have at least two types of branches (an axon and dendrites); glial cells have only one type of branch.
◆ Neurons can generate action potentials; glial cells cannot.
◆ Neurons have synapses that use neurotransmitters; glial cells do not have chemical synapses.

Myelin is a special tissue produced by some glial cells (Figure 1.3). Myelin wraps itself around some axons. This

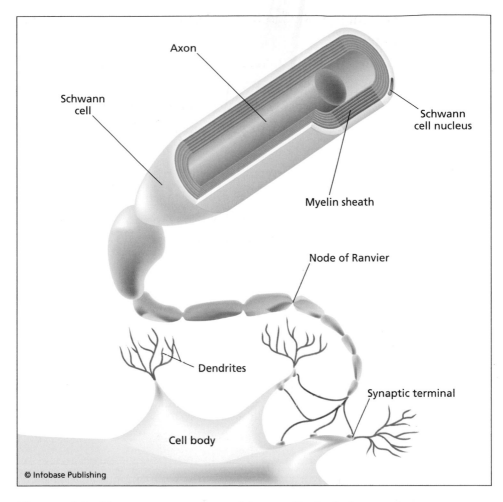

Figure 1.3 **Neurons are wrapped in myelin to help messages move quickly down the axon.**

wrapping helps electrical signals move down the axon at faster speeds. However, myelin does not cover the entire axon. Instead, there are small spaces in the myelin wrapping. These breaks in the myelin insulation are called **nodes of Ranvier**. Action potentials travel down an axon wrapped with myelin by jumping from node to node. This is called saltatory conduction. Therefore, information travels faster in axons that are insulated than in those that are not insulated with myelin.

Activities to Exercise Your Brain

SIMPLE NEURON MODEL

Here is a very simple neuron model that does not require any supplies. Use your hand and arm! Your hand is the cell body (also called the **soma**) of a neuron. Your fingers are dendrites that bring information to the cell body. Your arm is an axon taking information away from the cell body.

Materials
◆ None

• • • • •

BEADY NEURON

Get out those beads and make a neuron! This beady neuron with seven dendrites requires 65 beads: 42 beads for the den-

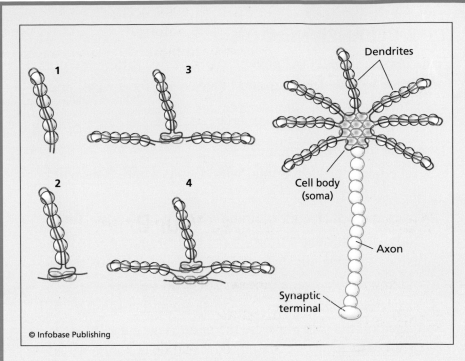

Figure 1.4 Model for a beady neuron.

dritcs, 10 beads for the cell body, 12 beads for the axon, and 1 bead for the synaptic terminal. String the beads using the pattern in Figure 1.4. The string can be yarn or rope, but for thc best result, usc flexible wire.

Materials

- ◆ 65 beads (4 different colors)
- ◆ 4 feet of string, yarn, rope, or flexible wire

PIPE CLEANER NEURON

This neuron model uses pipe cleaners of five different colors: one color for the dendrites and other colors for the cell body, axon, myelin sheath, and synaptic terminal.

Build the pipe cleaner neuron:

1 Take one pipe cleaner and wind it into a ball. This will be the cell body.
2 Take another pipe cleaner and attach it to the new "cell body" by pushing it through the ball so there are two halves sticking out. Take the two halves and twist them together into a single branch. This will be the axon.
3 Take other pipe cleaners and push them through the "cell body" on the side opposite the axon. These are the dendrites. The dendrites can be shorter than the axon. Add more pipe cleaners to make more dendrites.
4 Wrap small individual pieces of pipe cleaner along the length of the axon. These will create the myelin sheath.
5 Wrap another small pipe cleaner around the end of the axon. This will be the synaptic terminal.

Materials

◆ Pipe cleaners (five different colors)

● ● ● ● ●

NEURON IN A BAG

An edible neuron? Make one box of Jell-O® or other brand of gelatin by following the directions on the box. After the

Jell-O® has cooled, pour it into a small plastic bag. Add fruits (canned fruit cocktail works well) and candies to the Jell-O® to represent the special structures of a neuron. For example, mandarin orange slices could be **mitochondria**; a cherry could be the nucleus; red and black string licorice could be microtubules and neurofilaments. The plastic bag can represent the cell membrane. Don't forget **ribosomes**, the **Golgi apparatus**, and **endoplasmic reticulum**. Make a legend of the cell to show how each food represents the different organelles. After all the organelles have been added, tie off the top of the bag with a twist tie and place the "cell" in the refrigerator. After the Jell-O® sets, have a neuron snack.

Materials

◆ Jell-O® (any flavor)
◆ Plastic bags (sandwich size)
◆ Canned fruit
◆ Candies
◆ Twist ties
◆ Paper or index card and pen for the legend

● ● ● ● ●

MESSAGE TRANSMISSION

Electrical signals (action potentials) can travel down an axon at speeds up to 268 miles/hr (431 km/hour). When these electrical signals reach the synaptic terminal, they cause the release of chemicals (neurotransmitters). The chemical messages cross the synapse to transmit a message from one neuron to another neuron. Make a chain of neurons by forming a line of several people. Each person in the line will be a neuron. Each person should be at arm's length from the next person. Left hands and fingers are the dendrites of a neuron, bodies are cell bodies, right arms are axons, and right hands are synaptic terminals. Each person should hold a small vial of liquid (or some other item) in his or her right hand. When someone says "go," the person at the beginning of the line should start the signal transmission by placing his or her "neurotransmitter" into the left hand of the adjacent person. Once this message is received, this second neuron places its neurotransmitter into the dendrites of the next neuron. The third neuron then places its neurotransmitter into the dendrites of the next neuron and the "signal" travels to the end of the line. The transmission is complete when the "signal" goes all the way to the end of the line.

Remember that each "neuron" will pass its own transmitter to the next neuron in line. Each neuron has its own supply of neurotransmitter.

Materials

◆ Small containers of colored water (or other small item)

• • • • •

SALTATORY CONDUCTION—HAVE A BALL!

Action potentials travel down a myelin-covered axon by jumping from node to node. This is called **saltatory conduction**. Because the action potential jumps from node to node, the speed of transmission increases. To model saltatory conduction, play "Have a Ball." Divide players into two equal teams. Players from each team should line up behind one another. Players on each team should be separated from another player by 2 to 3 feet. Each player represents a node of Ranvier along a myelinated axon. The first player (the first "node") of each team is given a ball. The ball represents the action potential. When someone says "go," the first player must bend over and pass the ball through his or her legs to the next player. This next player must keep the ball moving by passing the ball through his or her own legs to the next player in line. The ball should travel through the legs of all players until it gets to the last player. In this way, the ball (the "action potential") will jump from person to person ("node to node") as it makes its way down the line of players (the "axon").

Materials

◆ Ball (one for each team)

• • • • •

ALL OR NONE

Use this game of All or None to model the "all or none" principle of action potentials. With chalk, mark off one area to represent a synaptic terminal and another area about 20 feet away to represent a dendrite and cell body. Divide players into two or more teams. Each player (except one on each team) will be a neurotransmitter waiting inside the synaptic terminal of a neuron (neuron #1). One player on each team stays ready inside of another neuron (neuron #2); this player is the action potential. When someone says "go," the neurotransmitters from each team leave the synaptic terminal of neuron #1, cross the synaptic gap, and run toward neuron #2. Knotted ropes representing receptors surround neuron #2. There should be one rope for each player who will be neurotransmitters (Figure 1.5). When the neurotransmitter players reach neuron #2, they must untie the knots in their ropes. Untying the rope represents binding of a neurotransmitter with a receptor. When the knots are untied, each rope is placed inside of neuron #2. When all the ropes are untied and placed in the neuron, the player who was waiting inside of the neuron runs down the neuron, down the axon, to the end. This represents the firing of the action potential. The action potential cannot start until all of the ropes are untied and placed inside of the neuron. The first team to get its action potential to the end of neuron #2 is the winner.

In this game:
- Players in synaptic terminal of neuron #1 = neurotransmitters
- Player in neuron #2 = action potential
- Ropes = receptors on neuron #2
- Untying rope = receptor binding
- Running down the neuron = the "all or none" action potential

Materials

- Large space
- Ropes
- Chalk (to mark off areas)

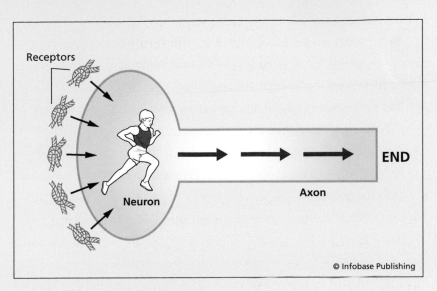

Figure 1.5 Illustration of All or None game.

ROPE NEURON

This giant model of a neuron illustrates the properties of chemical transmission and the action potential. You must construct the neuron before you use it with a group of people. Cut 2- to 3-foot lengths of rope to use as dendrites. Another 10- to 15-foot piece of rope will be turned into the axon. The cell body and synaptic terminal of the neuron can be plastic containers. Make holes in the plastic containers for the dendrites and axon. To secure the dendrites and axon in place, tie a knot in the ropes so they will not slip through the holes of the containers. The action potential is modeled with a pool float. Thread the pool float onto the axon before you secure the axon in place. Place small plastic balls or ping-pong balls in the synaptic terminal and your model is ready to go!

Set up the model:

1 Volunteers should hold each of the dendrites.
2 One volunteer should hold the cell body and one should hold the synaptic terminal. Make sure the person holding the synaptic terminal keeps his or her hands AWAY from the place where the axon attaches.
3 Another volunteer should hold more molecules of neurotransmitter (more plastic balls) near the people who are the dendrites.
4 Get one volunteer to hold the action potential.

Use the model:

1 The person holding the neurotransmitter molecules should toss the plastic balls to the people who are dendrites. The "dendrite people" try to catch the plastic balls. This models the release of neurotransmitters and the attachment (binding) of neurotransmitters to receptors on dendrites.
2 When three plastic balls are caught by dendrites, the person holding the action potential can throw/slide the pool float down the axon. This simulates the depolarization of the neuron above its threshold value and the generation of an action potential.
3 The action potential (pool float) should speed down the axon toward the synaptic terminal where it will slam into the container. This should cause the release of the neurotransmitters (plastic balls) that were being held there.

If the entire model is stretched tightly, the pool float should travel down to the terminal smoothly. This model can be used to reinforce the "all or none" concept of the action potential:

- Once the action potential starts, it continues without interruption.
- The size of the action potential stays the same as it travels down the axon.

Materials

- Rope (for dendrites and axon)
- Plastic containers (for cell body and synaptic terminal)
- Pool float (or another object that will slide along the rope; for the action potential)
- Plastic balls (for neurotransmitters)

2

Parts of the
Nervous System

There are billions of neurons in the nervous system that must work together for your body to work properly. The nervous system can be divided into two connected systems that function together: the **central nervous system** and the **peripheral nervous system**.

CENTRAL NERVOUS SYSTEM

The central nervous system contains two parts: the brain and the spinal cord (Figure 2.1). The average adult human brain weighs about 3 pounds (1.4 kg) and the spinal cord weighs about 1.4 ounces (40 g). The brain is not like a bowl of Jell-O®. Unlike a bowl of Jell-O®, the brain does not look the same in every place. Some areas of the brain are packed with many neurons (nerve

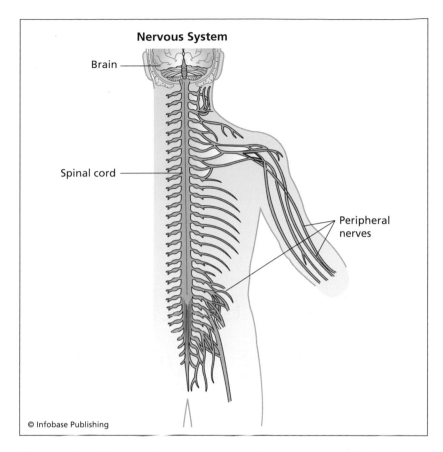

Figure 2.1 **The central nervous system consists of the brain and the spinal cord. The peripheral nervous system consists of nerves that relay information between the central nervous system and the distant parts of the body.**

cells) while other areas have few neurons. Areas of the brain that are densely packed with cell bodies look darker than areas with many axons.

When the brain is removed from the skull, it looks like a large pinkish-gray walnut. Each half of the brain is called a **hemisphere**. The right and left hemispheres are connected by a thick bundle of 200 to 300 million axons called the **corpus callosum**. The corpus callosum sends information between the two hemispheres. The **cerebral cortex** of each hemi-

Table 2.1 **AVERAGE BRAIN WEIGHTS**

Species	Weight (g)
Adult human	1,300-1,400
Sperm whale	7,800
Elephant	4,783
Giraffe	680
Horse	532
Chimpanzee	420
California sea lion	363
Lion	240
Grizzly bear	234
Sheep	140
Baboon	137
Dog (beagle)	72
Beaver	45
Cat	30
Rabbit	10-13
Alligator	8.4
Guinea pig	4
Owl	2.2
Rat	2
European quail	0.9
Bullfrog	0.24
Goldfish	0.097

sphere is divided into four lobes by various **sulci** and **gyri**. Sulci (or fissures) are the grooves and gyri are the bumps on the surface of the brain. The bumps and grooves of the cerebral cortex cause folds in the brain. These folds increase the surface area of cerebral cortex that can fit inside the skull. Although the patterns of gyri and sulci on the brains of different people are similar, no two brains are exactly alike.

The four lobes of the cerebral cortex are the frontal lobe, the parietal lobe, the temporal lobe, and the occipital lobe (Figure 2.2). The frontal lobe is located at the front of the brain and is involved with reasoning, planning, parts of speech, movement, emotions, memory, and problem-solving. The parietal lobe is located behind the frontal lobe and is involved with the perception of information related to touch, pressure, temperature, and pain. The temporal lobe is located below the parietal lobe and frontal lobe and is involved with the perception and recognition of auditory information (hearing) and memory. The occipital lobe is located at the back of the brain, behind the parietal lobe and temporal lobe, and is involved with vision.

The major parts of the brain include the cerebral cortex, cerebellum, thalamus, hypothalamus, brain stem, limbic system, and the basal ganglia. These are presented in more detail below.

The cerebral cortex (or cerebrum) is responsible for thought, voluntary movement, language, memory, reasoning, and perception. The word "cortex" comes from the Latin word for "bark" (of a tree). The cortex is a sheet of tissue that makes up the outer layer of the brain. The thickness of the cerebral cortex varies from .08 to .24 inches (2 to 6 mm).

The **cerebellum** is located behind the **brain stem**. It is similar to the cerebral cortex in that it is divided into hemispheres

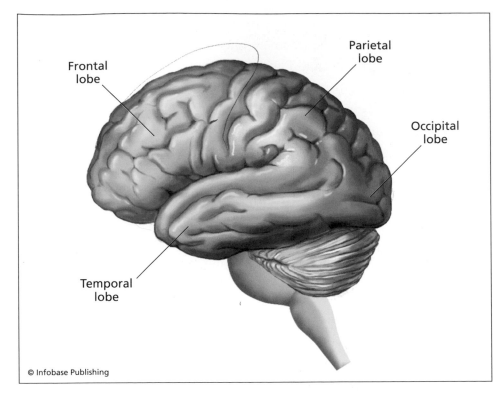

Figure 2.2 **The brain consists of four sections, or lobes. Functions of the body, such as vision, speech, and movement, can often be pinpointed to specific locations within the lobes.**

and has a cortex that surrounds its hemispheres. Its functions include coordinating and generating movement, balance, and posture.

The **thalamus** receives sensory information and relays this information to the cerebral cortex (Figure 2.3). The thalamus also receives information from the cerebral cortex, which it relays to other areas of the brain. The thalamus is also involved with movement.

Body temperature, emotion, hunger, thirst, and **circadian rhythms** are regulated by the **hypothalamus**, a pea-sized area

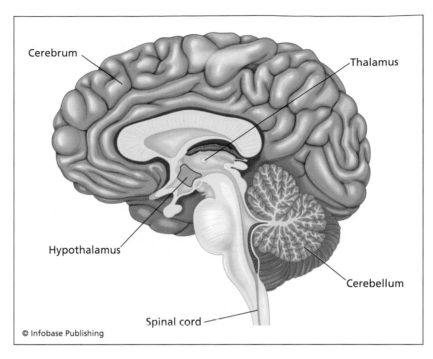

Figure 2.3 **The thalamus serves as a relay station for information to and from the cerebral cortex. Just below the thalamus is the hypothalamus, which helps regulate body temperature, hunger, and thirst. The hippocampus and amygdala are part of the limbic system, which is involved with emotional behavior and memory.**

located at the base of the brain. The hypothalamus acts as a "thermostat" by sensing changes in body temperature and then sending signals to adjust the temperature. For example, if the hypothalamus detects increases in body temperature, it sends signals to expand small blood vessels in the skin. This cools the blood faster. The hypothalamus also controls the release of **hormones** from the pituitary gland.

The brain stem is the term given to the area of the brain between the thalamus and the spinal cord. Structures within the brain stem include the medulla, pons, tectum, reticular formation, and tegmentum. Some areas of the brain stem are responsible for the most basic life functions, such as breathing and maintaining heart rate and blood pressure.

The **limbic system** (or the limbic areas) is a group of structures that includes the amygdala, **hippocampus**, mammillary bodies, and cingulate gyrus. These areas are important for controlling the emotional response to a given situation. Many of these areas are also important for memory and learning.

The **basal ganglia** are a group of structures that include the globus pallidus, caudate nucleus, subthalamic nucleus, putamen, and substantia nigra. These structures are important for coordinating movement.

THE SPINAL CORD

The spinal cord is the main pathway for information connecting the brain and peripheral nervous system. The spinal column, made of bones called **vertebrae**, protects the spinal cord. Although the spinal column is somewhat flexible, some of the vertebrae in its lower parts are joined. The spinal cord is made up of 31 segments: 8 cervical, 12 thoracic, 5 lumbar, 5 sacral, and 1 coccygeal (listed from top to bottom). A pair of spinal nerves exits from each segment of the spinal cord.

The spinal cord is approximately 18 in (45 cm) long in men and 17 in (43 cm) long in women. The length of the spinal cord is much shorter than the length (28 in [70 cm]) of the bony spinal column. In fact, the spinal cord extends down to only the first lumbar vertebra.

Receptors in the skin respond to stimuli such as pressure and temperature. These receptors send information to the spinal cord through the spinal nerves. The cell bodies for the neurons that make up the spinal nerves are located in the dorsal root ganglion. Axons of the spinal nerves enter the spinal cord through the dorsal root. Some axons make synapses with neurons in the dorsal horn, whereas others continue up to the brain. Many cell bodies in the ventral horn of the spinal cord send axons through the ventral root to muscles to control movement.

There are differences in the shape and size of the spinal cord at different levels. The darker color in each segment represents **gray matter**. The shape of the gray matter looks similar to the letter "H" or a butterfly (Figure 2.4). High concentrations of nerve cell bodies are located in the gray matter. Surrounding the gray matter is **white matter** (lighter color shading). The axons of neurons in the spinal cord are located in the white matter.

Facts About Backbones

The world's largest invertebrate (animal without a backbone) is the giant squid (*Architeuthis dux*). The giant squid can grow up to 60 feet (18 m) long and weigh up to 2,000 pounds (900 kg). The world's smallest vertebrate (animal with a backbone) is the stout infantfish (*Schindleria brevipinguis*). This fish is found in the coral lagoons in eastern Australia. Infantfish grow to approximately 0.30 inches (8 mm), live for only two months, and do not have any teeth or scales.

Source: "Tiniest Vertebrate," *Science*. Vol. 305 (July 23, 2004): p. 472.

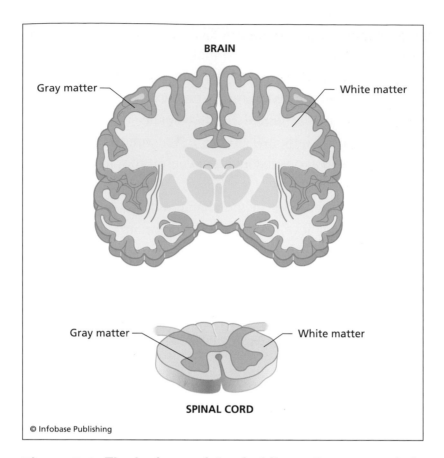

BRAIN

Gray matter

White matter

Gray matter

White matter

SPINAL CORD

© Infobase Publishing

Figure 2.4 The brain consists of white matter surrounded by gray matter, while the spinal cord consists of gray matter surrounded by white matter.

The relative amount of gray and white matter differs at each level of the spinal cord. In cervical segments, there is a relatively large amount of white matter. This pattern is caused by the many axons going up to the brain from all levels of the spinal cord and because there are many axons traveling from the brain down to different segments of the spinal cord. In lower segments of the spinal cord, there is less white matter because there are fewer axons traveling to and from the brain.

There are also differences in the gray matter. In some cervical segments, the ventral horn (the lower half of the segment) is enlarged. In some lumbar segments, the ventral horn is also large. These segments are those that contain motor neurons that control movement of the arms (cervical segment) and legs (lumbar segment).

BRAIN DEVELOPMENT

The brain grows at an amazing rate as it develops. At times during brain development, 250,000 neurons are added every minute! By the time a child is two years old, he or she has a brain that is approximately 80% the size of an adult's brain (Figure 2.5).

Although people have most of the neurons they will ever have when they are born, the brain continues to grow. The brain gets larger as glial cells continue to divide and multiply and as neurons make new connections. It was once thought that neurons in the adult brain did not replace themselves when they died or became damaged. However, research now shows that at least one part of the adult brain (the hippocampus) maintains its ability to make nerve cells.

The nervous system develops from embryonic tissue called **ectoderm**. The first sign of the developing nervous system is the neural plate. The neural plate can be seen at approximately the sixteenth day of development. Over the next few days, a trench is formed in the neural plate. This trench creates a neural groove. By the twenty-first day of development, a neural tube is formed when the edges of the neural groove meet. The rostral (front) part of the neural tube goes on to

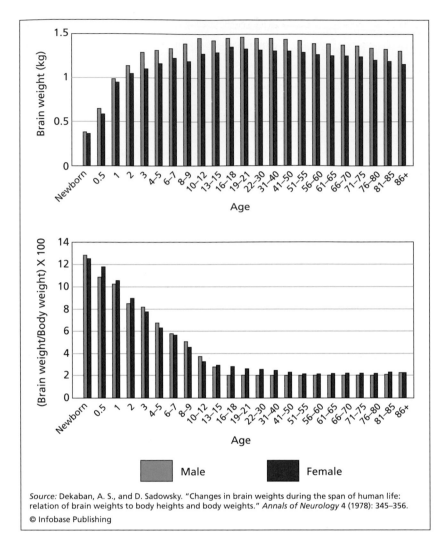

Source: Dekaban, A. S., and D. Sadowsky. "Changes in brain weights during the span of human life: relation of brain weights to body heights and body weights." *Annals of Neurology* 4 (1978): 345–356.

© Infobase Publishing

Figure 2.5 The top graph shows the brain weights of males and females at different ages. The bottom graph shows the brain weight to total body weight ratio (expressed as a percentage). The adult brain makes up approximately 2% of the total body weight, while a newborn's brain makes up approximately 13% of the total weight.

develop into the brain and the rest of the neural tube develops into the spinal cord. Neural crest cells become the peripheral nervous system.

At the front end of the neural tube, three major brain areas are formed: the prosencephalon (forebrain), mesencephalon (midbrain) and rhombencephalon (hindbrain). By the seventh week of development, these three areas divide again. This process is called **encephalization**.

PERIPHERAL NERVOUS SYSTEM

Nerves that extend out of the brain and spinal cord are part of the peripheral nervous system. Some of these nerves bring information into the central nervous system from the senses (sensory nerves), whereas other nerves take information away from the central nervous system to control muscles or glands (motor neurons). Some peripheral nerves have both sensory and motor functions.

The peripheral nervous system is divided into two major divisions: the **somatic nervous system** and the **autonomic nervous system**.

The somatic nervous system is made up of nerves that send sensory information into the central nervous system and nerves that send information from the central nervous system to skeletal muscles. The autonomic nervous system is divided into three parts: the **sympathetic nervous system, parasympathetic nervous system**, and **enteric nervous system**. The autonomic nervous system controls smooth muscle of the **viscera** (internal organs) and glands. The enteric nervous system is a third division of the autonomic nervous system that you do not hear much about. The enteric nervous system is a network of nerves that innervate the viscera (gastrointestinal tract, pancreas, gall bladder).

CRANIAL NERVES

The **cranial nerves** are 12 pairs of nerves on the ventral (bottom) surface of the brain (Figure 2.6). These nerves bring information from the sense organs to the brain, control muscles, or are connected to glands or internal organs.

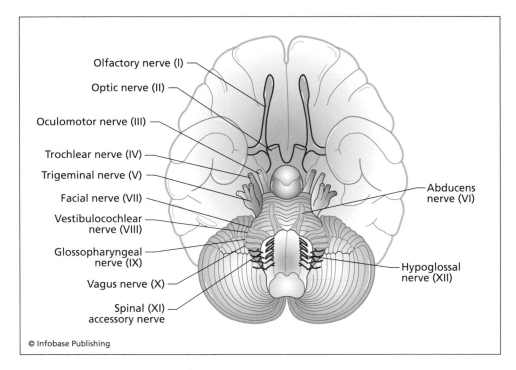

Olfactory nerve (I)

Optic nerve (II)

Oculomotor nerve (III)

Trochlear nerve (IV)

Trigeminal nerve (V)

Facial nerve (VII)

Vestibulocochlear nerve (VIII)

Glossopharyngeal nerve (IX)

Vagus nerve (X)

Spinal (XI) accessory nerve

Abducens nerve (VI)

Hypoglossal nerve (XII)

© Infobase Publishing

Figure 2.6 The cranial nerves are connected to the brain stem. They control sensory and muscle functions in the eyes, face, throat, and abdomen.

Table 2.2 **CRANIAL NERVES**

Number	Name	Function
I	Olfactory nerve	Smell
II	Optic nerve	Vision
III	Oculomotor nerve	Eye movement; pupil size
IV	Trochlear nerve	Eye movement
V	Trigeminal nerve	Somatosensory information (touch, pain) from the face and head; muscles for chewing
VI	Abducens nerve	Eye movement
VII	Facial nerve	Taste (anterior 2/3 of tongue); somatosensory information from ear; controls muscles used in facial expression
VIII	Vestibulocochlear nerve	Hearing; balance
IX	Glossopharyngeal nerve	Taste (posterior 1/3 of tongue); touch information from tongue, tonsil, pharynx; controls some muscles used in swallowing
X	Vagus nerve	Sensory, motor and autonomic functions of viscera (glands, digestion, heart rate)
XI	Spinal accessory nerve	Controls muscles used for head movement
XII	Hypoglossal nerve	Controls tongue muscles

COVERINGS OF THE BRAIN AND SPINAL CORD

There are several layers of tissue that separate your brain from the outside world. First, there is skin (scalp). Beneath the skin is bone (skull). Three special coverings called the **meninges** are located under the skull.

The outer layer of the meninges is called the **dura mater**. The dura is tough and thick and restricts the movement of the brain within the skull. This protects the brain from movements that may stretch and break brain blood vessels. The middle layer of the meninges is called the **arachnoid**. The inner layer, the one closest to the brain, is called the **pia mater**. To remember the order of the meninges, just learn: "The meninges PAD [**p**ia; **a**rachnoid; **d**ura] the brain."

VENTRICULAR SYSTEM AND CEREBROSPINAL FLUID

The entire surface of the central nervous system is bathed by a clear, colorless fluid called **cerebrospinal fluid (CSF)**. CSF in the brain is also contained within a system of fluid-filled cavities called **ventricles** (Figure 2.7). The choroid plexus, a tissue in the lateral, third, and fourth ventricles, produces CSF. CSF flows from the lateral ventricle to the third ventricle through the interventricular foramen (also called the foramen of Monro). The third ventricle and fourth ventricle are connected to each other by the **cerebral aqueduct** (also called the aqueduct of Sylvius). CSF then flows into the subarachnoid space through the foramina of Luschka (there are two of these) and the foramen of Magendie (only one of these).

Absorption of the CSF into the bloodstream takes place in the superior sagittal sinus through structures called arachnoid villi. When the CSF pressure is greater than the venous pressure, CSF flows into the blood stream. The arachnoid villi act as one-way valves. If the CSF pressure is less than the venous

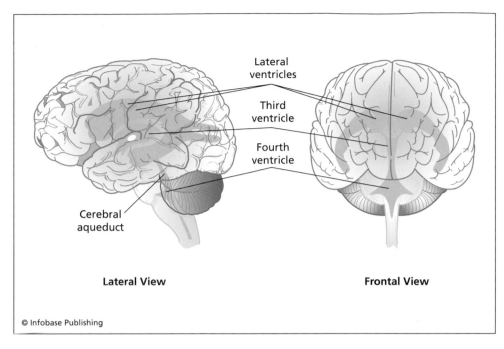

Lateral ventricles

Third ventricle

Fourth ventricle

Cerebral aqueduct

Lateral View

Frontal View

© Infobase Publishing

Figure 2.7 **The ventricular system consists of four cavities, or ventricles, which produce cerebrospinal fluid.**

pressure, the arachnoid villi will not let blood pass into the ventricular system.

The CSF has several functions, including:

1 **Protection**: CSF protects the brain from damage by "buffering" the brain. In other words, CSF cushions a blow to the head and lessens the impact.

2 **Buoyancy**: Because the brain is immersed in fluid, the net weight of the brain is reduced from approximately 3 pounds (1.4 kg) to approximately one-tenth of a pound (50 g). Therefore, pressure at the base of the brain is reduced.

3 **Excretion of waste products**: The one-way flow from the CSF to the blood takes potentially harmful chemicals away from the brain.

4 **Endocrine medium for the brain**: CSF transports hormones to other areas of the brain. Hormones released into the CSF can be carried to remote sites of the brain where they may act.

Activities to Exercise Your Brain

MODELING THE BRAIN

Use a black marker to draw an outline of the brain on the outside of a white swimming cap. Draw lines to divide the brain into its four lobes. Color each lobe of the brain.

Materials
- White swimming cap
- Black marker
- Color markers

BRAIN COMPARISONS

How is the brain similar to other objects? For example, how is the brain like a bowl of Jell-O®? How is it different? Are they both soft? Do they have layers? Can they store information? Do they use electricity? Do they contain chemicals? Make a list of similarities and differences between different objects and a brain.

Materials

◆ Suggested objects—balloon, Jell-O®, tape recorder, apple, camera, computer, telephone, book, ball, cauliflower, cooked noodles, calculator, paper, spider web, map, tree, river, toolbox, dictionary, computer

● ● ● ● ●

BRAIN CHARADES

Although it is not too difficult to describe what the brain does, it is not always easy to act out these functions. Try to describe the functions of the brain and nervous system with this game of "Brain Charades." Write down words that describe brain functions on small pieces of paper. Here is a list of words to get started:

Vision	Smell	Taste	Touch	Hearing
Emotions	Movement	Memory	Speech	Heart rate
Breathing	Thinking	Planning	Sleep	Reading
Balance	Eating	Drinking	Dreaming	Body rhythms

Mix the papers in a bowl, bag, or hat. A player should pick a paper out of the bowl then act out the function. Everyone else should try to guess what the player is acting out. Actors must remain silent. After someone guesses the action, another player should select a new word and act it out. Repeat the game until all of the words have been identified correctly.

Materials

◆ Paper
◆ Pen or pencil
◆ Container for words

● ● ● ● ●

EMOTION NOTION

Happy? Sad? Mad? Surprised? Make an "Emotion Collage" by cutting out magazine pictures of people expressing different emotions. Glue the pictures on a piece of paper or make a poster to show the different emotions. Separate papers or posters each showing a different emotion can also be made.

Materials

◆ Magazines with pictures of people
◆ Scissors
◆ Glue
◆ Paper or poster board

MAKE THE BONES OF THE SPINAL COLUMN

The human spinal cord is protected by the bony spinal column. There are 31 segments of the spinal cord and 33 bones (vertebrae) that surround these segments. There are 7 cervical vertebrae, 12 thoracic, 5 lumbar, 5 sacral, and 4 coccygeal vertebrae in the human body. To model these bones, get 33 empty spools of thread (buttons may also work). Run a string or thread through the middle of one of the spools or buttons. Tie off one end of the string and put the remaining spools or buttons on the string. Each spool (or button) represents one vertebra. When the model is finished, notice how it can bend. In a real spinal column, ligaments hold the vertebrae together.

Materials

◆ Empty thread spools or buttons
◆ String

• • • • •

TEST THE CRANIAL NERVES

The following tests illustrate how the cranial nerves work. Each test requires two people: one person will be the experimenter (tester) and the other will be the test subject. The experimenter should record what the subject says and does.

Olfactory Nerve (I)
    Gather some items with distinctive smells (for example, cloves, lemon, chocolate, or coffee). Your partner should

close his or her eyes and smell the items one at a time with each nostril. Can your partner identify the smells?

Optic Nerve (II)

Borrow or make an eye chart. It does not have to be perfect. Can your partner read the lines at various distances away from the chart?

Oculomotor Nerve (III), Trochlear Nerve (IV), and Abducens Nerve (VI)

These three cranial nerves control eye movement and pupil diameter. Hold up a finger in front of your partner. Tell your partner to hold his or her head still and to follow your finger when you move it up and down, right and left. Do your partner's eyes follow your finger?

Check the pupillary response (oculomotor nerve): look at the diameter of your partner's pupils in dim light and also in bright light. Check for differences in the sizes of the right and left pupils.

Trigeminal Nerve (V)

The trigeminal nerve has sensory and motor functions. To test the motor part of the nerve, tell your partner to close his or her jaws as if he or she was biting down on a piece of gum. To test the sensory part of the trigeminal nerve, lightly touch various parts of your partner's face with a piece of cotton or a blunt object. Be careful not to touch your partner's eyes. Can your partner feel the touch?

Facial Nerve (VII)

The motor part of the facial nerve can be tested by asking your subject to smile, frown, or make funny faces. The sensory part of the facial nerve is responsible for taste on the front two-thirds of the tongue. Put a few drops of sweet or salty water on this part of the tongue. Can your partner taste this flavored water?

Vestibulocochlear Nerve (VIII)

Although the vestibulocochlear nerve is responsible for hearing and balance, test only the hearing portion of the nerve. Have your partner close his or her eyes. At what distance can your partner hear the ticking of a clock or stopwatch?

Glossopharyngeal Nerve (IX) and Vagus Nerve (X)

Have your partner drink some water and watch for the swallowing reflex. The glossopharyngeal nerve is also responsible for taste on the back one-third of the tongue. Place a few drops of sweet or salty water on this part of the tongue to see if your partner can taste it.

Spinal Accessory Nerve (XI)

Test the strength of the muscles used in head movement by putting your hands on the sides of your partner's head. Tell your subject to move his or her head from side to side. Apply only light pressure when the head is moved. Can your partner move his or her head without a problem?

Hypoglossal Nerve (XII)

Have your partner stick out his or her tongue and move it side to side. Can your partner move his or her tongue?

● ● ● ● ●

BE A MOVIE CRITIC

Here is a chance to watch a movie and learn something about the brain at the same time. The assignment is to watch a movie about the brain or senses. Such movies include *The Boy Who Could Fly*, *Charly*, *Quest for Camelot*, *Mr. Holland's Opus*, and *The Miracle Worker*. Write a short report about how the nervous system was involved in the movie.

● ● ● ● ●

BRAIN RÉSUMÉ

Pick a job, any job. Pretend a brain was going to interview for this job. Why would this brain be best for the position? What parts of the brain are best for the job? Develop a résumé (a summary of qualifications, experience, and education) for the brain. Choose an occupation. For example, why is the brain best suited for a teacher? Why is the brain best suited for a basketball player? What would the brain of a lawyer, fire fighter, or a police officer look like?

BRAIN TRAVEL GUIDE

Someone wants to take a trip to the brain. What will they find there? What does each part do? What can people do at each location? Write a travel guide for the brain explaining what someone can see and do when they visit the brain.

• • • • •

CREATE A "BRAINY" NEWSPAPER

Create and publish a brainy newspaper. Add the names of the writers, headlines, and stories about a day in the life of the brain. For example, call the newspaper "The Daily Dendrite" or "The Brain Bulletin." Stories might include:

◆ "The Hippocampus Goes to Work"—Describe how the hippocampus was used during a lesson at school (for example, by transferring short-term memories into long-term memories).

◆ "Visual Cortex Sees All"—Describe how the visual cortex responded during a field trip.

◆ "Cerebellum Goes Into Overtime"—Describe how the cerebellum was used during a basketball game.

Other stories could include how the brain stem, the senses, and the autonomic nervous system were used.

3

Functions of the Nervous System

The nervous system receives signals from the outside world (and from inside the body) through the senses. The brain must process this information, make decisions, and send signals to muscles, internal organs, and glands to react to these messages. The nervous system also interacts with other systems of the body such as the skeletal, circulatory, muscular, digestive, and respiratory systems. Although each system has specific functions, they are all interconnected and dependent on one another. The brain receives information from many organs of the body and adjusts signals to these organs to maintain proper functioning.

SIDEDNESS

How many brains do you have? One or two? You really have only one brain, but the cerebral hemispheres are divided down the middle into a right hemisphere and a left hemisphere. The hemispheres communicate with each other through the corpus callosum.

Approximately 90% of the population is right-handed. Right-handed people prefer to use their right hand to write, eat, and throw a ball. People who prefer to use their right hand are also called "right-hand dominant." It follows that most of the other 10% of the population is left-handed or "left-hand dominant" although there are a few people who are able to use each hand equally; they are said to be **ambidextrous**.

The right side of the brain controls muscles on the left side of the body and the left side of the brain controls muscles on the right side of the body (Figure 3.1). In general, sensory information from the left side of the body crosses over to the right side of the brain and information from the right side of the body crosses over to the left side of the brain. Therefore, damage to one side of the brain will affect the opposite side of the body.

In 95% of right-handers, the left side of the brain is dominant for language. The left side of the brain is also used for language in 60% to 70% of left-handers. In the 1860s and 1870s, neurologists Paul Broca and Karl Wernicke observed that people who had damage to a particular area on the left side of the brain had speech and language problems. People with damage to these areas on the right side of the brain usually did not have any language problems. These two areas of

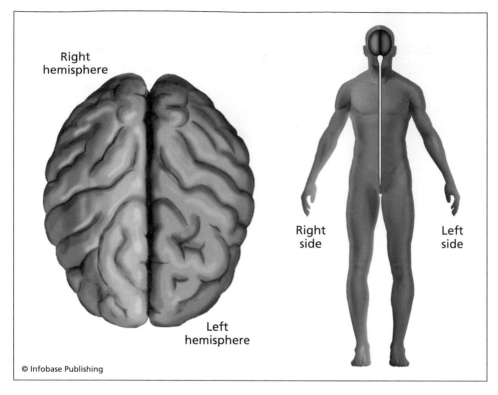

© Infobase Publishing

Figure 3.1 **The brain is divided into left and right hemispheres. The left hemisphere controls motor skills of the right side of the body and the right hemisphere controls the left side of the body.**

the brain that are important for language now bear the names of these neurologists: **Broca's area** and **Wernicke's area**.

RIGHT SIDE/LEFT SIDE

People have dominant parts of their bodies for many jobs. Approximately 90% of the population is right-handed: These people prefer to use their right hand for most tasks. People

Table 3.1

Percentage of Men and Women Who Use the Right Side		
	Men	**Women**
Hand	86	90
Foot	77	86
Ear	55	65
Eye	73	69
Source: Stanley Coren, *The Left-Hander Syndrome: The Causes and Consequences of Left-Handedness*, New York: Free Press, 1992, p. 32.		

are also right- or left-footed, and some even prefer to use one of their ears over the other.

MOVEMENT AND REFLEXES

Reflexes are automatic movements that take place when something affects our senses. For example, if an area just below your kneecap is tapped, your leg will kick out (Figure 3.2). You don't have to think about kicking your leg—it happens automatically. Many reflexes, such as the knee-jerk reflex, do not require the brain. The entire reflex circuit is located within the peripheral nervous system and spinal cord. Reflexes occur quickly to prevent injuries to our bodies.

 ## SLEEP AND DREAMING

We spend approximately 8 hours each day, 56 hours each week, 240 hours each month, and 2,920 hours each year

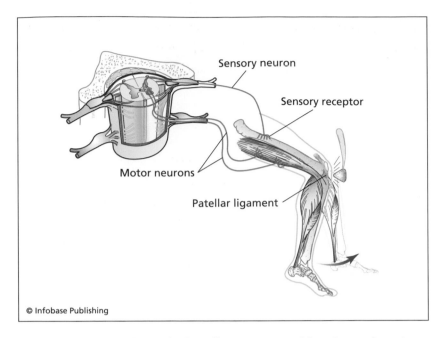

Figure 3.2 **The knee-jerk reflex occurs without any input from the brain. When the area just below the kneecap is tapped with a mallet, sensory neurons transmit a signal to the spinal cord. The signal is then relayed to the quadriceps muscle, which contracts and causes the leg to kick up.**

doing it. Sleeping, that is! For one third of our lives, we are asleep, seemingly doing nothing. But is sleep really a time when nothing happens? It certainly looks like it. Our eyes are closed, our muscles are relaxed, our breathing is regular, and we don't react to sound or light. A look inside the brain reveals a different situation, however: The brain is very active.

Scientists can record the electrical activity of the brain by attaching electrodes to the scalp. These electrodes are connected to a machine called an **electroencephalograph**. The

electroencephalogram (or EEG) is the record of brain activity recorded with this machine. The wavy lines of the EEG are what most people know as brain waves.

STAGES OF SLEEP

Sleep follows a regular cycle of activity each night. The EEG pattern changes in a predictable way several times during the night. There are two basic forms of sleep: slow wave sleep (SWS) and **rapid eye movement (REM) sleep**. Infants spend approximately 50% of their sleep time in SWS and 50% in REM sleep. Adults spend approximately 20% of their sleep time in REM and 80% in SWS sleep. Elderly people spend less than 15% of their sleep time in REM sleep.

REM AND SWS SLEEP

During REM sleep, a person's eyes move back and forth rapidly. Most dreaming happens during REM sleep. Sleep researchers discovered this when they woke people up during REM sleep. Often, people can remember their dreams if they are awakened during REM sleep. The EEG pattern during REM sleep is similar to the EEG pattern when people are awake. However, muscle activity is very low during REM sleep. Muscles are inactive during REM sleep so that we will not act out our dreams. SWS sleep is made up of four different stages (stage 1, stage 2, stage 3 and stage 4), each with a different EEG pattern.

While we are asleep, our brains ride a roller coaster through different stages of sleep. As we drift off to sleep, we first enter stage 1 sleep. After a few minutes, the EEG changes to

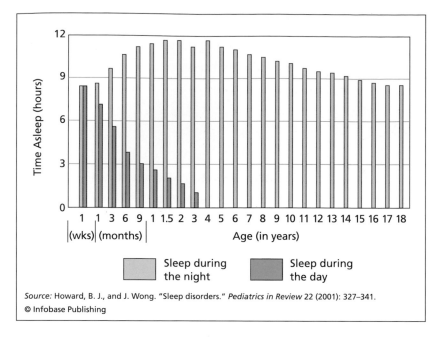

Source: Howard, B. J., and J. Wong. "Sleep disorders." *Pediatrics in Review* 22 (2001): 327–341.
© Infobase Publishing

Figure 3.3 Newborns sleep equally during the daytime and nighttime. By four years old, most children sleep entirely at night.

stage 2 sleep, then stage 3 sleep, and then stage 4 sleep. Then it is back up again: stage 3, stage 2, and then a period of REM sleep. Then back down again, and back up again, and down again. The brain cycles through these stages approximately four or five times during an eight-hour period of sleep.

Sleep patterns change as people age (Figure 3.3). Newborn babies sleep approximately 16 hours each day and spend approximately 50% of that time in REM sleep. Older people (50 to 85 years of age) sleep only 5.75 to 6 hours per day and spend roughly 15% of that time in REM sleep. The graph illustrates how nighttime and daytime sleep time changes as people age.

BIOLOGICAL RHYTHMS

Most animals coordinate their activities according to the daily cycles of light and dark. These cycles are called circadian rhythms from the Latin words "circa" meaning approximately and "dies" meaning day. One common circadian rhythm is activity: Some animals are active during the day (diurnal) and others are active during the night (nocturnal). Many body functions also follow a circadian rhythm. For example, body temperature and neurotransmitter levels cycle throughout the day.

MEMORY AND LEARNING

What's your name? How old are you? Where do you live? How do you ride a bike? The answers to these questions are in your brain. They are some of your memories and your memories are much of what makes you who you are.

Memories are formed when the brain receives information from our senses. This sensory information is stored in the brain for a very short time and most is not kept. If the information is kept, it goes into short-term memory. Short-term memory can hold approximately seven pieces of information. Short-term memories that are saved go into long-term memory. Long-term memories can last a lifetime. When information travels repeatedly along a particular pathway in the brain, connections between neurons get stronger. Learning and memories develop through these strong connections.

The part of the brain called the hippocampus is essential for moving information from short-term memory to long-term memory. The hippocampus is sometimes surgically removed to stop seizures in people who have epilepsy. Some people find it impossible to create new memories after they have this type of surgery. They can remember things that occurred before their surgery, but they cannot form new memories: Without the hippocampus, information cannot get from short-term memory to long-term memory.

MEMORY TECHNIQUES

Here are a few methods that may improve your ability to remember.

Visualization

Visualization is the ability to see an object in your mind. In general, strange or unusual images are easier to remember. For example, if you go to the mall and park a car on level C in space #5, you might imagine that there are five cats waiting in your car for your return. The "C" in the word "cats" helps you remember that the car is on level C and the five cats in your image helps you remember that the car is parked in space #5.

Chaining

Chaining is a form of visualization, but it includes remembering several objects in a specific order. You must link the objects together by thinking of images that connect them. Although a grocery list does not have to be remembered in order (although it sometimes helps to find things faster), let's use it as an example. Here is a short list of items from the store: milk, bread, eggs, cheese, orange juice. Now, chain these items together with images:

1 A carton of milk being poured on top of a loaf of bread
2 A sandwich (the bread) with raw eggs on it

3 Eggs stuck in the holes of a block of Swiss cheese

4 Pieces of cheese hanging from an orange tree

Try to chain this list of 20 words:

shoe-piano-tree-pencil-bird-bus-book-dog-pizza-flower-basketball-door-TV-rabbit-spoon-eye-chair-house-computer-rock

You may find that bizarre and wild associations are easiest to remember.

The Method of Loci

Location, location, location. The method of loci was created during the time of the Roman Empire. This memory technique uses a chaining method that links specific places in the order that you would visit them. For example, you might think of the route you take to school:

1 Your room (you wake up)

2 Your kitchen (you have breakfast)

3 Front door of your house

4 Bus stop

5 Bus seat

6 Friend's house that you see from the bus

7 Gas station that you see from the bus

8 Market that you see from the bus

9 School

Now you must link the items that you want remembered to each of these places. You have to remember the places first, of course, but this should be easy. Chain each item to a place on your route. Using the grocery store example, you might think of milk pouring on you in your room, bread that you can't get out of the toaster (kitchen), eggs splattered on your front door, etc.

Chunking

Have you ever wondered why phone numbers are listed as a three-digit number and a four-digit number and *not* as a single seven-digit number? It's 999-9999, not 9 9 9 9 9 9 9. What about social security numbers? It's 123-45-6789, not 1 2 3 4 5 6 7 8 9. Numbers are much easier to remember in small chunks. Try to create fewer pieces of information from multiple numbers. Which is easier to remember?

1 8 9 6 2 0 1 6 3 9 4 7

or

1896 2016 3947

Acrostics

An acrostic uses the first letters of words to create a phrase to help remember a list. Medical students often learn this one when they study neuroanatomy:

On Old Olympus' Towering Top A Famous
Vocal German Viewed Some Hops.

In this phrase, the first letter of each word represents the first letter of each of the cranial nerves, in order: olfactory nerve (I), optic nerve (II), oculomotor nerve (III), trochlear nerve (IV), trigeminal nerve (V), abducens nerve (VI), facial nerve (VII), vestibulocochlear nerve (VIII), glossopharyngeal nerve (IX), vagus nerve (X), spinal accessory nerve (XI), hypoglossal nerve (XII).

Here's another one:

My Very Early Morning Jam Sandwich
Usually Nauseates People
or
My Very Excellent Mom
Just Served Us Nine Pizzas

These two phrases represent the order of planets from the sun: Mercury, Venus, Earth, Mars, Jupiter, Saturn, Uranus, Neptune, Pluto

Activities to Exercise Your Brain

TESTING SIDEDNESS

Right Hand/Left Hand

Test people for handedness. Which hand do they prefer to use in the following tests?

1 Ask your subject to write his or her name. Which hand does your subject use to write?

2 Ask your subject to cut a circle out of a piece of paper. In which hand does your subject hold a pair of scissors when cutting a piece of paper?

3 Give a ball to your subject and ask him or her to throw it to you. Which hand does your subject use to throw a ball?

4 Observe which hand your subject uses to eat. You should only count the hand that is used to bring the food to your subject's mouth. Which hand holds the fork or spoon?

5 Observe which hand your subject uses to pick up a cup of water to drink.

Materials

◆ Pen or pencil and paper
◆ Paper and scissors
◆ Ball
◆ Fork or spoon and food
◆ Cup with water

Right Foot/Left Foot

Test people for "footedness." Which foot do they prefer to use in the following tests?

1 Place a ball on the ground near your subject. Which foot does your subject use to kick the ball?

2 Have your subject stand with both feet flat on the ground in front of a step. Ask your subject to step up the first stair. Which foot is lifted up on to the step? (If you do not

have any stairs, you can draw a line on the ground or put a piece of string on the ground.) Does your subject lead with the right or left foot? Ask your subject to step over the line or string. Which foot goes over the line?

3 Put a small object, such as a coin, on the floor. Ask your subject to step on the coin. Which foot does your subject use to step on the coin?

Materials

◆ Ball
◆ Stairs, chalk, or string
◆ Coin

Right Eye/Left Eye

Test people for "eyedness." Which eye do they prefer to use in the following tests?

1 Give your subject an empty paper towel tube (or a rolled up piece of paper). Ask your subject to look through the tube. Which eye does your subject use to look through a tube?

2 Ask your subject to look at a distant object across the room (such as a clock on the wall). Tell your subject to quickly line up one finger with the distant object so that this finger is blocking the object. Now ask your subject to close one eye, then the other. When your subject closes one eye, the object will remain blocked. However, with the other eye, your subject's finger will "jump" out of the

way. Which eye does your subject "sight" with? Note the eye that blocks the object.

3 Cut a small circle out of the middle of a piece of notebook paper. The circle should be the size of a small coin. Give the paper with the hole to your subject. Ask your subject to keep both eyes open and to look through the hole in the paper at a distant object (such as a clock on the wall). Ask your subject to bring the paper closer and closer to his or her face while still looking at the distant object. Which eye does the hole in the paper finally reach?

Materials

◆ Paper or cardboard tube
◆ Paper with small hole

Right Ear/Left Ear

Test people for "earedness." Which ear do they prefer to use in the following tests?

1 Tell your subjects that you are going to whisper something very quietly and that you want them to cup one ear to make the sound louder. Speak quietly. Which ear do your subjects use?

2 Get a small box and ask your subjects to pretend that something is inside of it. Ask your subjects how they would identify what is inside the box by putting an ear up to the box. Which ear do your subjects use?

3 Ask your subjects to try to listen through a wall. Which ear do your subjects use?

Materials

◆ Small box

Collect and Analyze Your Results

For each subject, determine if all of the responses were on the right side, left side, or mixed. For example, did your subject use his or her right hand for all of the handedness tests? If there are more right-sided responses than left-sided responses, you can call that person right-handed. Do the same for the foot, ear, and eye. Is your subject right- or left-handed? Right- or left-footed? Right- or left-eyed? Right- or left-eared?

Summarize the data from all of your subjects:

◆ How many people in your test were right-handed? How many were left- handed?

◆ How many people in your test were right-footed? How many were left-footed?

◆ How many people in your test were right-eyed? How many were left-eyed?

◆ How many people in your test were right-eared? How many were left-eared?

◆ Does it make a difference if your subject was a boy or girl? How many boys were right-handed? How many girls?

Compare your data to that in the table on page 53, which were collected from another experiment. How do your numbers compare?

• • • • •

PUPIL TO PUPIL (PUPILLARY REFLEX)

Dim the lights in a room. After a few minutes, look at the eyes of another person and observe the size of his or her pupils (the black center spot in the middle of the eye). Turn the room lights back on. Check the size of the pupils again. The pupils should now be smaller. This is the pupillary response: It keeps out excessive light automatically.

Materials

◆ Room with lights

• • • • •

THINK FAST! (BLINK REFLEX)

Blinking is another built-in reflex. Have someone stand behind a see-through barrier such as a window or a wire screen. Throw a cotton ball at the person. Did the person blink? Probably. The blink reflex protects our eyes from damage.

Materials

◆ Cotton balls
◆ Screen (wire or glass)

HOW FAST ARE YOU?

This project does not involve a simple reflex. Rather, this activity is designed to measure the time necessary to respond to something that is seen. Get a ruler (or a yardstick). Hold the ruler near the end (highest number) and let it hang down. Have another person put his or her hand at the bottom of the ruler. This person should be ready to grab the ruler, but they should not be touching the ruler. Tell the person that the ruler will be dropped sometime within the next five seconds and that they are supposed to catch the ruler as fast as they can after it is dropped. Record the level (inches or centimeters) at which they catch the ruler. Convert the distance into reaction time with the chart below. Test the same person three to five times. Vary the time you drop the ruler within the five-second "drop-zone" so the other person cannot guess when the ruler will be dropped.

This reaction time experiment requires that the brain receives visual information (the movement of the ruler). The brain then sends a motor command ("grab that falling ruler") to the muscles of the arm and hand. If all went well, the ruler was caught.

Use table 3.2 to convert the distance on the ruler to reaction time. For example, if the ruler is caught at the 8-inch mark, then the reaction time is equal to 0.20 seconds (200 ms). Remember that there are 1,000 milliseconds (ms) in 1 second.

Table 3.2 **CONVERTING DISTANCE TO REACTION TIME**

Distance of Catch	Reaction Time
2 in (~5 cm)	0.10 sec (100 ms)
4 in (~10 cm)	0.14 sec (140 ms)
6 in (~15 cm)	0.17 sec (170 ms)
8 in (~20 cm)	0.20 sec (200 ms)
10 in (~25.5 cm)	0.23 sec (230 ms)
12 in (~30.5 cm)	0.25 sec (250 ms)
17 in (~43 cm)	0.30 sec (300 ms)
24 in (~61 cm)	0.35 sec (350 ms)
31 in (~79 cm)	0.40 sec (400 ms)
39 in (~99 cm)	0.45 sec (450 ms)
48 in (~123 cm)	0.50 sec (500 ms)

• • • • •

KEEP A "SLOG" (A SLEEP/DREAM LOG)

A great way to study sleep is to keep a daily record of your dreams. Keep a pen, pencil, and paper near your bed. Record the day and time you go to bed. When you wake up record your dreams immediately because details about dreams fade with time. Also, record the time that you wake up. Write down as many details about your dream that you can remember. With practice, you may be able to improve your memory so you can remember more details of your dreams.

In your dream report, consider:

1 Are your dreams in color?
2 Does your dream have a "sense of time?"

3 Were you emotional in your dream? Were other people emotional?

4 How many different dreams can you remember for one night of sleep?

5 Do the same people, events, or places recur in your dreams?

6 Do some of the events that occurred during the day appear in your dreams?

7 Do thoughts that you had before going to sleep reappear in your dreams?

8 Does watching a movie or a TV show before you go to bed influence what you dream about?

9 Does eating certain foods during the day influence your dreams?

10 Does your mood affect your dreams?

11 Are your dreams on weekdays different than your dreams on the weekends?

12 Does the time of year influence your dreams?

13 Does the time when you go to sleep influence your dreams?

14 Are your nighttime dreams different than the dreams you have during naps?

15 Are your dreams different when you are sick or take medicine?

16 Have you ever had the same dream more than once?

17 Is your memory of a dream better if you wake up naturally or when you use an alarm clock?

18 Are your dreams similar to those of other people?

Materials

◆ Paper, pen/pencil

DROP OFF OR DRIFT OFF?

Most people do not drift off to sleep gradually. Rather, the change from being awake to being asleep is very quick. It is similar to switching off a light. To investigate if this is true for you, turn on a TV or radio as you are going to sleep. Keep the volume low. When you wake up, ask yourself if the TV or radio gradually faded out or if suddenly, everything just went blank. What was the last thing you remember before you fell asleep?

Materials

◆ TV or radio

● ● ● ● ●

BE AN REM DETECTIVE

REM is an abbreviation for rapid eye movement sleep. Sleep laboratories use expensive equipment to monitor brain waves for REM sleep, but even without this equipment you can be a sleep researcher. During REM sleep, a person's eyes move back and forth. Although most people's eyes are closed (or partially closed) when they are sleeping, you can still detect movement of their eyeballs through their eyelids.

You should practice observing eye movements with some-one who is awake. Ask the person to close and then move his or her eyes. You should see a bulge moving behind the eyelid quite easily. Now you are ready to do some sleep research. When someone is sleeping, take a peek at his or her eyes.

Can you see the eyes moving back and forth rapidly? If so, the person is probably in REM sleep. There are only approximately four or five REM periods in one night's sleep, so you might miss it.

Materials

◆ None

• • • • •

SLEEP LATENCY

How long does it take to fall asleep? Dr. William C. Dement in his book, *The Promise of Sleep* (1999), describes a way to measure the time it takes to fall asleep. Write down the time you get into bed. When you are in bed, hold a metal spoon over a plate on the floor. When you fall asleep, your muscles will relax and the spoon will fall out of your hand. The noise of the spoon hitting the plate should wake you up. Write down the time you woke up. The difference between the time you got into bed and time you woke up is your sleep latency. If the spoon misses the plate, you may not wake up. If this happens, use a large metal cookie sheet instead of a plate.

Materials

◆ Spoon
◆ Plate (or cookie sheet)
◆ Clock (or timer)

THE UPS AND DOWNS OF BODY TEMPERATURE

Body temperature is a circadian rhythm that is easy to track. Get an oral thermometer such as the one you use when you are sick. Make sure you know how to use it properly and do not use one that contains mercury. Measure your temperature every two hours from the time you get up in the morning to the time you go to sleep. Do not eat or drink anything right before you take your temperature. Make sure to take your temperature the same way every time and that you read the temperature accurately. Differences in your body temperature vary by only a few tenths of a degree. Chart your body temperature with time using graph paper. Label the x-axis as "Time of Day" and y-axis as "Body Temperature." Does your body temperature change with the time of day? Is there a pattern?

Materials

◆ Thermometer
◆ Graph paper

● ● ● ● ●

RHYTHMS ALL AROUND

All animals have biological rhythms. You can study cycling patterns in animals if you have a pet such as a rat, rabbit, hamster, fish, cat, dog, or frog. For example, if you have a rat, you can observe the amount of time it spends eating, walking, and sleeping at different times of the day. Check on your pet every two hours and watch it in 10-minute periods. If you work with a group of people, each person should observe one type of behavior. For example, one person can measure the amount of time the animal spent eating and another person can watch for sleeping. Do not disturb the animal while you are observing it. Chart the amount of time the animal spends in each behavior at different times of the day. Keep track of it for several days. Are there any consistent patterns?

Materials

◆ Animal
◆ Graph paper
◆ Stopwatch

• • • • •

NOW YOU SEE IT, NOW YOU DON'T

This is a test of short-term memory. Get a tray or a large plate. Put 10 to 20 objects on the tray, and cover them with a towel or cloth. Tell other people that you have a number of objects on the tray and that you want them to remember as many items as possible. Also tell them that they will have only one minute to view the objects. Remove the cover from the tray and start the timer. After one minute, cover the tray. Ask the people to write down all the items they can remember. Can they remember all of the items? Are there any items that everyone forgets?

Materials

◆ Tray or plate
◆ Timer

◆ 10 to 20 small items (such as an eraser, pencil, coin, marble, etc.)
◆ Cloth or towel to cover the tray
◆ Paper and pencils for people to write down what they remember

• • • • •

WHAT'S MISSING

This experiment is a variation of the previous short-term memory experiment. Get your tray, items, and cloth ready again. This time have people view the items for one minute. Cover the tray again. Remove one item from the tray. Show the tray and remaining items to the people again. Ask them, "What is missing?" Can they identify the object you removed?

Repeat the experiment with some changes:

1 Give people more (or less) time to view the items.
2 Use more objects on the tray.
3 Use fewer objects, but have the people identify the missing object by feeling the remaining objects without seeing them.
4 Remove three or four objects.

Materials

◆ Tray or plate
◆ 10 to 20 small items (such as an eraser, pencil, coin, and marble)
◆ Cloth or towel to cover the tray

ROOM MIX-UP

Tell everyone to take a good look around a room filled with people. Ask them to remember where objects are located in the room. Then send a few people out of the room while you change the location of various objects in the room. When the people come back, ask them to write down all of the things that have changed. Make sure you keep a master list of all the things that you have changed!

Materials

- At least 10 people
- Room filled with different objects

• • • • •

SHAPE UP!

Have you wondered how animals are trained to do tricks in the circus or on TV? One way that trainers teach animals to learn new things is through a method called shaping. This technique involves reinforcing the animal for each behavior that looks similar to the final act you want. In other words, the trainer gives the animal a treat each time the animal does something that looks similar to the final behavior.

Now it's your turn to shape a friend. Get a collection of "treats." These treats could be pebbles, pennies, jellybeans, or buttons. Without telling your friend the exact behavior you would like to see, just say that you will give him or her a treat when he or she does the right thing. The final behavior might be to turn off a light or pick up a pencil or open a book.

Let's say the final behavior you are looking for is to have your friend turn off a light. Start giving treats when your friend stands up. Give another treat when your friend starts to walk. Give another treat when your friend gets close to the light and another when your friend touches the light. Give one more treat when your friend turns off the light. Do not give treats for behaviors that are not related to turning off the light.

You can shape almost any behavior as long as your friend is interested in getting the treat.

Materials

- Treats (such as pennies, small candies, jellybeans, buttons, cereal pieces)

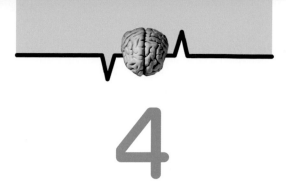

4

The Senses

Your senses are your windows to the outside world. They gather information to tell you what is going on in the ever-changing environment. Special cells in your ears, eyes, mouth, nose, and skin send signals to your brain to help you understand what is happening. Your brain analyzes this information and sends signals to control muscles and glands to react to what is happening. We use our senses to find out:

◆ *What* is in the environment?
◆ *How much* is out there?
◆ Is there *more* or *less* of it than before?
◆ *Where* it is?
◆ Is it *changing* in time or place?

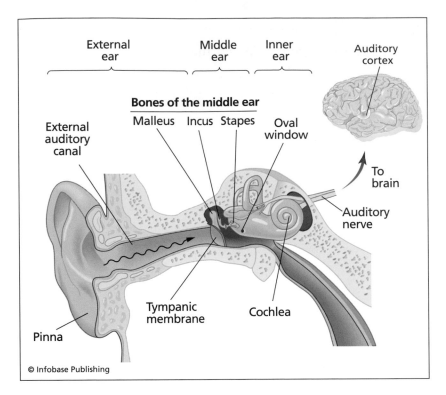

External ear | Middle ear | Inner ear | Auditory cortex

Bones of the middle ear

Malleus Incus Stapes

Oval window

External auditory canal

To brain

Auditory nerve

Tympanic membrane

Cochlea

Pinna

© Infobase Publishing

Figure 4.1 The ear is a complex organ made up of many specialized parts. These parts work together to generate nerve impulses that are carried to the brain by the auditory nerve.

HEARING

Sound waves enter the outer ear and cause the **tympanic membrane** (eardrum) to vibrate. The three bones in the middle ear (**malleus, incus, stapes**) pass these vibrations to the cochlea. The **cochlea** is a snail-shaped, fluid-filled structure in the inner ear (Figure 4.1). Inside the cochlea is another structure called the organ of Corti. Hair cells are located on the **basilar membrane** of the cochlea. **Cilia** (the hair) of the hair cells make contact with another membrane called the tectorial membrane. When the hair cells are moved by vibration, a nerve impulse is generated in the auditory nerve. These impulses are then sent to the brain.

SMELL

Your appreciation of the smells of a rose, perfume, freshly baked bread, and cookies are made possible by your nose and brain. The sense of smell, called **olfaction**, involves the detection and perception of chemicals floating in the air. Chemical molecules enter the nose and dissolve in mucus within a membrane called the **olfactory epithelium**. In humans, the olfactory epithelium is located approximately 3 inches (8 cm) up and into the nose.

The olfactory epithelium contains hair cells that respond to particular chemicals (Figure 4.2). These receptor cells have small hairs called cilia on one side and an axon on the other side. Humans have approximately 40 million olfactory receptors; a German shepherd has approximately two billion olfactory receptors.

No one knows what causes olfactory receptors to react, but it may be related to a molecule's shape, size, or electrical charge. The electrical activity produced in hair cells is sent to the olfactory bulb. The information is then passed on to mitral cells in the olfactory bulb. The olfactory tract transmits the signals to brain areas such as the olfactory cortex, hippocampus, amygdala, and hypothalamus. These brain areas are part of the limbic system. The limbic system is involved with emotional behavior and memory. That is why certain smells often bring back memories associated with the object.

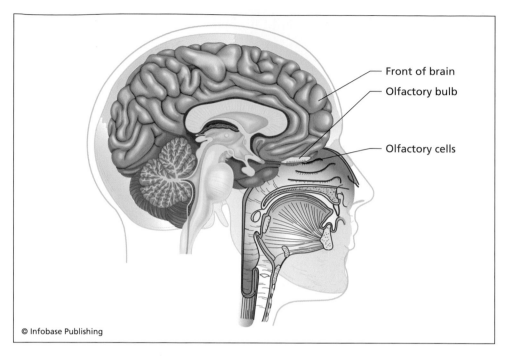

Front of brain
Olfactory bulb
Olfactory cells

© Infobase Publishing

Figure 4.2 Cells of the olfactory (smell) system respond to chemicals by producing electrical signals that are carried to the olfactory bulb. The olfactory tract transmits the signals to brain areas such as the olfactory cortex, hippocampus, amygdala, and hypothalamus.

If you have ever had a cold, then you know that you cannot smell very well when your nose is stuffed up. This is because the molecules that carry smell cannot reach the olfactory receptors.

TASTE

Delicious, scrumptious, delectable, mouth-watering, yummy, stale, awful, terrible, unsavory, bland, unpalatable: just a few of the many words used to describe how food tastes. The scientific word for the sense of taste is **gustation**.

For food to have a taste, it must be dissolved in water. Saliva in our mouths helps dissolve food. Most people recognize four common basic tastes: sweet, salty, sour, and bitter. A fifth basic taste called **umami** has also been discovered. Umami is the taste of foods that contain glutamate (such as monosodium glutamate, parmesan cheese, sardines, and sweet soy sauce). Different parts of the tongue can detect all of the basic tastes. All other tastes come from a combination of the basic tastes.

The organ of taste is the taste bud. Each taste bud (there approximately 10,000 taste buds in humans) is made up of 50 to 150 receptor cells. Receptor cells live for only one or two weeks and then are replaced by new receptor cells.

Sensitive Senses

An "absolute threshold" is the stimulus intensity that a person can detect 50% of the time. Examples of absolute thresholds for the five senses are:

- Vision: a candle flame, 30 miles away, on a dark, clear night
- Hearing: A ticking watch 20 feet away in a quiet place
- Taste: A teaspoon of sugar in two gallons of water
- Smell: a drop of perfume in a three-room apartment
- Touch: The wing of a bee falling from 1 centimeter onto your cheek

Source: R.S. Feldman, *Understanding Psychology*, 4th edition, New York: McGraw-Hill, 1996, p. 98.

Each receptor in a taste bud responds best to one of the basic tastes. A receptor can respond to the other tastes, but it responds strongest to a particular taste.

Two cranial nerves in the tongue carry taste information: the facial nerve (cranial nerve VII) and the glossopharyngeal nerve (cranial nerve IX). The facial nerve is responsible for taste from the anterior (front) two thirds of the tongue and the glossopharyngeal nerve is responsible for taste from the posterior (back) third of the tongue. Another cranial nerve (the vagus nerve, X) carries taste information from the back part of the mouth. The cranial nerves send taste information into a part of the brain stem called the nucleus of the solitary tract. From the nucleus of the solitary tract, taste information goes to the thalamus and then to the cerebral cortex. Taste information also goes to limbic areas such as the hypothalamus and amygdala. Another cranial nerve (the trigeminal nerve, V) is also located in the tongue, but is not used for taste. Rather, the trigeminal nerve carries information related to touch, pressure, temperature, and pain.

TOUCH

Your skin is a giant, washable, stretchable, tough, waterproof sensory apparatus that covers your whole body. Weighing between 6 and 10 pounds (3 to 4 kg) and having a surface area of approximately 20 square feet (1.85 square meters), your skin keeps your insides in! The outside layer of your skin is called the epidermis; the inside layer is called the dermis.

There are four different types of skin:

1 Mucocutaneous skin: skin at the junction of the mucous membrane, hairy skin, lips, and tongue.

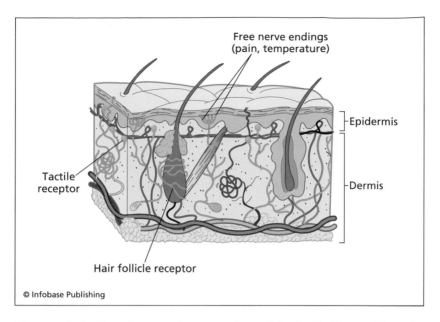

Figure 4.3 **Touch receptors are found in both the epidermis (upper layer) and dermis (lower layer) of the skin.**

2 Mucous membranes: linings of the inside of body orifices.

3 Glabrous skin: skin without hair; the epidermal layer is 1.5 mm thick; the dermis is 3 mm thick.

4 Hairy skin: skin with hair; the epidermal layer is 0.07 mm thick; the dermis is 1 to 2 mm thick.

Information from your skin allows you to identify distinct types of sensations such as tapping, vibration, pressure, pain, heat, and cold. For you to make these distinctions, your skin has different types of sensory receptors that respond best to different types of mechanical, thermal, or chemical energy (Figure 4.3). These receptors send information to your brain where you perceive these signals.

VISION

We are very visual animals. We use our sense of sight to interpret much of the world around us. What we see is called light. Light is part of the electromagnetic radiation spectrum that includes X-rays, ultraviolet radiation, and radio waves. Humans can see only a small part of the electromagnetic radiation spectrum—the part that has wavelengths between 380 and 760 nanometers. These wavelengths are visible light. Our eyes do not have detectors for wavelengths less than 380 or greater than 760 nanometers. Therefore, we cannot see other types of energy such as ultraviolet light or radio waves. Rattlesnakes, however, can detect electromagnetic radiation in the infrared range. These snakes can "see" heat and use this ability to find prey. Some insects such as honeybees can see into the ultraviolet range.

Animal Eyes

Not all eyes are created equal. Consider the following facts about animal eyes:

- Unlike humans, the octopus does not have a blind spot.
- The "four-eyed" fish (*Anableps*) has two pupils in each of its eyes. Therefore it can see above and below the water simultaneously.
- Each eye of a dragonfly has about 30,000 lenses.
- Squid and cuttlefish have eyes with W-shaped pupils.
- The giant squid has the largest eyeball of any living animal. The diameter of its eyeball is ten inches, which is about ten times the size of a human eyeball.

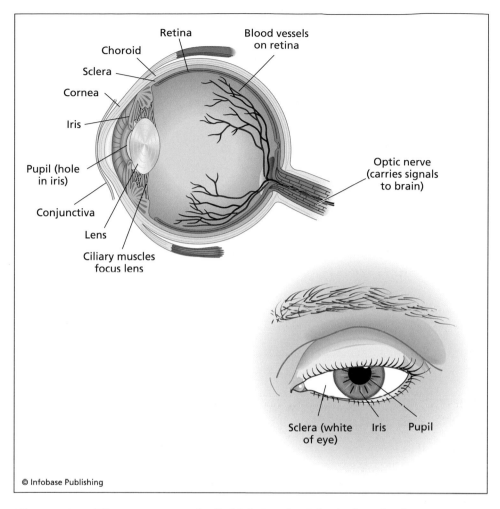

Figure 4.4 **The eye converts light into electrical signals that are carried by the optic nerve to the brain.**

THE EYE

The human eye is approximately 1 inch (2.5 cm) in length and weighs approximately 0.25 ounces (7 g). Light passes through the **cornea**, **pupil**, and **lens** before it reaches the **retina**. The **iris** is a muscle that controls the size of the pupil and therefore the amount of light that enters the eye (Figure 4.4). The iris also determines the color of the eye. The vitreous or **vitreous humor** is a clear gel that provides constant pressure to maintain the shape of the eye. The retina is the area at the back of the eye that contains **photoreceptors** (light-

Table 4.1 **PARTS OF THE EYE**

Structure	Function
Aqueous humor	Clear, watery fluid found in the anterior chamber of the eye.
Choroid	Layer of blood vessels that nourish the eye; also, because of the high melanocyte content, the choroid acts as a light-absorbing layer.
Cornea	Transparent tissue covering the front of the eye. It does not have any blood vessels, but it does have nerves.
Iris	Circular band of muscles that control the size of the pupil. The pigmentation of the iris gives color to the eye. Blue eyes have the least amount of pigment; brown eyes have the most.
Lens	Transparent tissue that bends light passing through the eye. To focus light, the lens can bend to change shape.
Pupil	Hole in the center of the eye through which light passes.
Retina	Layer of tissue on the back part of the eye that contains cells responsive to light (photoreceptors).
Rods	Photoreceptors responsive in low-light conditions.
Cones	Photoreceptors responsive to color and in bright conditions.
Sclera	Protective coating around the back five-sixths of the eyeball.
Vitreous humor	Clear, jelly-like fluid found in the back portion of the eye that helps to maintain the shape of the eye.

sensitive cells) called **rods** and **cones**. These receptors generate electrical impulses when they are stimulated by light. The electrical signals travel out of the eye in the optic nerve and are sent to the brain.

Six bands of muscles attach to the eyeball to control the ability of the eye to look up and down and side to side. These muscles are controlled by three cranial nerves. Four of these muscles are controlled by the oculomotor nerve (cranial nerve III), one muscle is controlled by the trochlear nerve (cranial nerve IV), and one muscle is controlled by the abducens nerve (cranial nerve VI).

Rods are most sensitive to light and dark changes, shape, and movement. They contain only one type of light-sensitive pigment. Rods are not good for color vision. In a dim room, we use mainly our rods, but we cannot see color. Rods are more numerous than cones at the edges of the retina. If you want to see a dim star at night, use your peripheral vision because you will be using your rod vision. There are approximately 120 million rods in the human retina.

Cones are not as sensitive to light as the rods. Each cone is most sensitive to one of three different colors (green, red, or blue). Signals from the cones are sent to the brain and translated into the perception of color. Because cones work in bright light only, it is difficult to see color in dark places. Cones are used for color vision and are also better suited for detecting fine details. There are approximately 6 million cones in the human retina.

The **fovea** is the area of the retina that provides the clearest vision. In the fovea, there are only cones and no rods. Cones are also packed closer together in the fovea than in the rest of the retina. Blood vessels and nerve fibers go around the fovea so light has a direct path to photoreceptors.

THE BLIND SPOT

The blind spot is an area on the retina that lacks photoreceptors and thus is unable to respond to light. This area contains the optic nerve, which exits the eye on its way to the brain. An image that falls on this part of the retina will not be seen.

—Activities to Exercise Your Brain —

MYSTERY NOISES

Test the ability of people to identify several sounds with this game. One person should be the "sound maker" who will collect several sound-making objects. Everyone else should close their eyes or turn away from the sound maker. The sound maker should make a sound and see if people can identify it. Example sounds:

- ◆ Shake pennies or other coins
- ◆ Clap hands
- ◆ Clap chalkboard erasers
- ◆ Tap a pencil or pen on a desk

- Close a book
- Crumple up paper or foil
- Stomp on the floor
- Tear some paper
- Close a stapler
- Bounce a ball

Materials

- Coins
- Pencil or pen
- Book
- Paper
- Foil
- Ball
- Stapler

• • • • •

MODEL EARDRUM

It's easy to make a model of the eardrum (also called the "tympanic membrane") and see how sound travels through the air. Stretch a piece of plastic wrap over a large bowl or pot (any container with a wide opening will work). Make sure the plastic wrap is stretched tightly over the container. The plastic represents the eardrum. Place 20 to 30 grains of uncooked rice on the top of the plastic wrap. Now you need a noise maker. A tin cookie sheet or baking tray works well. Hold the cookie sheet close to the plastic wrap. Hit the cookie sheet to create a "big bang" noise and watch the rice grains jump.

The "big bang" produces sound waves (changes in air pressure) that cause the plastic sheet to vibrate. The vibration causes the rice grains to move. Sound waves vibrate the eardrum in much the same way.

Materials

- Plastic wrap
- Container with wide opening
- Uncooked rice (any other small grain will work)
- Tin cookie sheet (or other noise maker)

•   •   •   •   •

SMELL MATCH

Collect pairs of items with distinctive odors and place them in opaque containers. Poke holes into the top of the containers. Mix up the containers and try to match the containers that have the same item. When you have made your decisions, open up the containers and see if you found a match.

Materials

- Suggested smells: lemon, orange peel, cedar wood, banana, pine needles, chocolate, coffee, dirt, vanilla, garlic, mint, vinegar, mothballs, onion, rose petals
- containers

TASTY BUDS

Taste buds on the tongue are, of course, important for the sense of taste. Are different parts of the tongue most sensitive to different basic tastes such as salty, bitter, sour, and sweet, or are all parts of the tongue equally sensitive to the tastes? Get samples of foods for each basic taste, for example, salty water, sugary water, vinegar, or lemon for a sour taste and onion juice for a bitter taste. Place each sample in a small container, cup, or bowl.

Dip a toothpick into one of the solutions or take up a small amount of solution into an eyedropper. Lightly touch the toothpick or use the eyedropper to put a small amount of solution on the tongue of your partner. Ask your partner if he or she can taste the solution and how strong the solution tasted. Repeat the tests on different portions of the tongue and with different solutions. It may help if your partner drinks some plain water between tests. Also be careful when you test the back part of the tongue because some people may gag. Draw a map of the tongue indicating the parts that are sensitive to the different tastes. Compare the tongue maps of different people. Can all parts of the tongue detect all flavors?

Materials

- Salt taste: salty water
- Sugar taste: sugary water
- Sour taste: lemon juice
- Bitter taste: onion juice or tonic water
- Toothpicks or eyedropper

◆ Containers for solutions
◆ Colored pencils and paper to draw a tongue map

• • • • •

THE NOSE KNOWS

The nose is important for the flavor of food. To demonstrate this, blindfold a partner. Have your partner hold his or her nose. Give your partner something to taste such as a pear or apple slice. Can he or she tell the difference between the pear slice and the apple slice? Baby foods are also good to use because they are made with a variety of fruit and vegetable flavors. You could also try different flavors of jelly beans. Have your partner try to guess the flavor with and without the use of his or her nose. Use foods that are the same texture so that the blindfolded person will not be able to use touch information to distinguish the different items.

Materials

◆ Foods to taste: fruit or vegetable slices, baby food, jelly beans
◆ Blindfold

• • • • •

TWO-POINT DISCRIMINATION

What area of the body is most sensitive to touch? Hands? Feet? Fingers? To find out, perform a two-point discrimination exam on a partner. Bend a paper clip into the shape of a U with the tips approximately ¾ of an inch (2 cm) apart. Make sure the tips of the U are even with each other. Lightly touch the two ends of the paper clip to the back of your partner's hand. Your partner should not look at the area of skin that is being tested. Do not press too hard! Make sure both tips touch the skin at the same time. Ask your partner if he or she felt one or two pressure points. If your subject reported one point, spread the tips of the clip further apart, then touch the back of the subject's hand again. If your subject reported two points, push the tips closer together, and test again.

Questions and comparisons

1 Try different parts of the body: arm, leg, fingers, back, neck, toes, hand, head.
2 Compare the distances required for an "I feel two points" response on different body regions.
3 What part of the body is most sensitive? In other words, where on the body can two points be detected with the smallest tip separation?

The receptors in our skin are not distributed equally on different parts of our bodies. Some places, such as our fingers and lips, have more touch receptors than other parts of our body, such as our backs. That is one reason why we are more sensitive to touch on our fingers and face than on our backs.

Materials

◆ Paper clips

SOCK IT TO ME!

Put small objects into each of several socks. Can people guess what is inside each sock by touching and feeling the object on the outside of the sock? If they cannot guess what the object is, have them put their hand into the sock and feel it. By touching the object, they can get more information about the characteristics (such as roughness and texture) of the object.

Materials

◆ Four to six socks
◆ Small objects to put into the socks: pencil eraser, coin, golf ball, rock, key chain

• • • • •

DEPTH PERCEPTION—I

Two eyes are better than one, especially when it comes to depth perception, or judging the distance between two objects. To demonstrate how two eyes are better than one to judge depth, hold the ends of two pencils, one in each hand. Hold them either vertically or horizontally facing each other at arms' length from your body. With one eye closed, try to touch the ends of the pencils together. Now try it using two eyes. It should be much easier because each eye looks at the image from a different angle. This experiment can also be done with your fingers, but pencils make the effect more dramatic.

Materials

◆ Pencils

DROP IT! DEPTH PERCEPTION—II

Here is another way to demonstrate the importance of two eyes for judging depth. Collect a set of pennies, buttons, or paper clips. Sit at a table with a partner. Put a cup about two feet away in front of your partner. Have your partner close one eye. Hold a penny in the air about two feet above the table. Move the penny around slowly. Ask your partner to say "Drop it!" when he or she thinks the penny will drop into the cup if you released it. When your partner says, "Drop it," drop the penny and see if it makes it into the cup. Try it again when your partner uses both eyes. Try it again with the cup farther away from or closer to your partner. Compare the results of 10 drops at each distance.

Questions

1 Is there improvement when your partner uses two eyes?
2 Is there improvement when the cup is closer to your partner?

Materials:

◆ Cup (yogurt cup or drinking cup)
◆ Drop objects (pennies, buttons, paper clips, clothespins)

● ● ● ● ●

TARGET PRACTICE

Draw a target similar to a "bull's-eye" on a large piece of paper (Figure 4.5). The actual dimensions of the circles are not too important and you do not have to color the circles.

Place the target on the ground about 5 feet (1.5 m) in front of you. Have a partner stand near the target. Give your partner an ink marker with the tip pointing down. Close one of your eyes. Tell your partner to move forward or backward or side-to-side until you think the marker would hit the center of the target if it was dropped. Tell your partner to drop the marker when you think the marker is over the target center. The marker should leave a spot where it hit the target. Try it

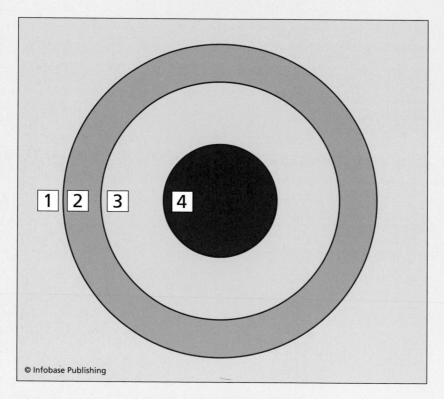

Figure 4.5 **An example of a bull's-eye target.**

10 times with one eye closed and add up the score for the 10 drops. Now try it with both eyes opened. Use a different color marker when you use two eyes to see the difference on the target. Is your score better when you use two eyes?

Materials

◆ Paper for target
◆ Markers (two colors)

● ● ● ● ●

STAR LIGHT, STAR BRIGHT

Have you noticed that it is easier to see a star in the sky when you do not look directly at it? It is easier to see a dim star by looking off to the side because the two types of photoreceptors (rods and cones) perform different functions and are located in different places in your retina. Cones are used for detail and color vision and are most numerous in the center of the retina. Rods work better in dim light and are most numerous at the sides of the retina. If you look off to the side of a star, the star's image will fall on an area of the retina that has more rods.

● ● ● ● ●

SEEING IN THE DARK

You cannot see in complete darkness, but you can see in dim light. In dim light, the rods in your eyes do most of the work. However, rods do not provide any information about color.

The other photoreceptors in your eye, called cones, are used for seeing color. Cones do not work in dim light. Therefore, you cannot see colors in dim light. To show how color is difficult to see in dim light, get five pieces of paper of different colors (colored typing paper or construction paper work well). Dim the lights until you can just barely see. Wait 10 minutes and then write on each paper the color that you think that paper is. Turn on the lights and see if your guesses were correct. Did you identify the colors correctly?

Materials

- Pencils or pens
- Colored paper (about five different colors)

5

The Health of Your Brain

Your brain is similar to a car. A car needs fuel, oil, brake fluid, and other materials to run properly. Your brain also needs special materials to run properly: glucose, vitamins, minerals, and other essential chemicals. The fuel (energy) for your brain is glucose. You can get glucose by eating carbohydrates or other foods that can be converted to glucose.

Your brain must manufacture the right proteins and fats to grow new connections and add myelin insulation to axons. To make these materials, you must digest proteins and fats in food and use the pieces (amino acids and fatty acids) to make the new brain proteins and fats. Your brain will not work properly if it does not have the correct amount and balance of particular building blocks. Too little or too much of a nutrient can affect the nervous system and other body systems.

Certain foods contain the starting materials for some neurotransmitters. If your diet does not have the necessary starting materials, your brain will not be able to make some neurotransmitters. Neurological and mental disorders can occur when neurotransmitter levels are unbalanced. The starting materials for some neurotransmitters include aspartic acid, choline, glutamic acid, phenylalanine, tryptophan, and tyrosine.

> **Aspartic acid**: Used to make aspartate; found in peanuts, pota-toes, eggs, and grains.
> **Choline**: Used to make acetylcholine; found in eggs, liver, and soybeans.
> **Glutamic acid**: Used to make glutamate; found in flour and potatoes.
> **Phenylalanine**: Used to make dopamine; found in beets, soy-beans, almonds, eggs, meat, and grains.
> **Tryptophan**: Used to make serotonin; found in eggs, meat, bananas, yogurt, milk, and cheese.
> **Tyrosine**: Used to make norepinephrine; found in milk, meat, fish, and legumes.

Nutrients must follow a specific pathway to your brain and overcome several challenges before they can be used:

1 They must gain entry to your body: If you do not eat them, they will not reach your brain.
2 Once in your stomach, they must survive an attack by acid that helps digest food.

3 Further along the digestive tract, they must be absorbed through the cells lining the intestine and transported through blood vessel walls into the bloodstream.
4 Traveling in the blood through the liver, nutrients must avoid being metabolized (destroyed).
5 Once in the bloodstream, nutrients must cross small blood vessels into brain tissue. The transportation of materials from the blood to neurons is restricted by the **blood-brain barrier (BBB)**.

The BBB keeps many substances out of the brain, but it also allows nutrients into the brain (Figure 5.1). The BBB is similar to a wall between the bloodstream and neurons: A substance must cross through this wall from the blood to reach neurons. The BBB can be crossed in three ways:

1 Through holes in the BBB.
2 By being transported through the BBB by special carriers.
3 By breaking down the BBB.

WHEN THINGS GO WRONG

Drugs, disease, and injury can all affect how the brain functions. Cocaine, LSD, heroin, marijuana, ecstasy, alcohol, nicotine, barbiturates, and rohypnol are some drugs that affect the neurotransmitter systems of the brain. These drugs can cause changes in a person's mood and thoughts and may result in addiction. Some drugs can even change, or possibly damage, the brain permanently. Head and spinal cord injuries can result in long-term damage to the nervous system. Almost half of all brain injuries are caused by motor vehicle accidents.

Many diseases of the brain can alter how a person moves, talks, thinks, and feels. Epilepsy, stroke, Parkinson's disease, Huntington's disease, Alzheimer's disease, amyotrophic lateral sclerosis (ALS, also known as "Lou Gehrig's disease" after a baseball player who contracted the disease), and cerebral palsy are just a few of the many neurological disorders that affect millions of people. Millions more people are affected by mental disorders such as depression and schizophrenia. These brain disorders take a tremendous emotional and economic toll on the people who are afflicted by these conditions.

BRAIN INJURY

Damaged brains are not easy to fix. Here are some suggestions for good brain health.

1   Wear your seat belt. In cars, trucks, or airplanes, your seat belt helps protect your brain from injury. Motor vehicle accidents are by far the greatest cause of brain injuries, accounting for 37% to 50% of all brain injuries.

2   Wear your helmet. When you bike, skate, snowboard, ski, or skateboard, your helmet protects your head if you fall. Make sure that your helmet meets or exceeds the American National Standards Institute (ANSI) and Snell Memorial Foundation standards for safety. If it does, it will be noted inside the helmet.

3   Stay away from illegal drugs. Drugs alter brain function. Although damage done by some drugs can be reversed, some drugs may change brain function permanently. Why take the chance?

4   Know the risks involved with sports. This applies mainly to sports such as boxing, football, and the martial arts, but even soccer, climbing, horseback riding, diving, and skiing have

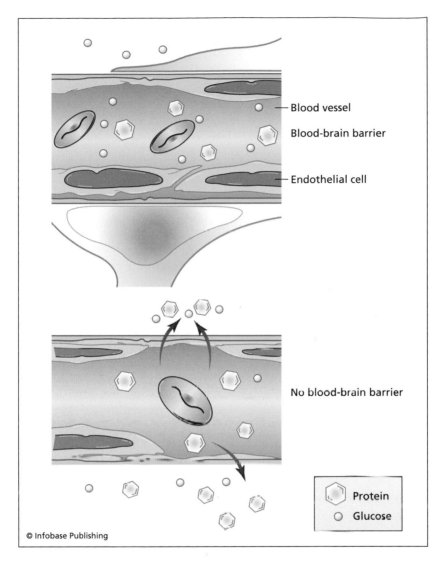

Figure 5.1 **The blood-brain barrier prevents the passage of large molecules, such as proteins, into the brain. Small molecules, such as glucose, are able to pass through the barrier.**

risks. Always wear your safety equipment properly and be in good physical condition for your sport.

5 Look before you leap. People can suffer brain and spinal cord injuries when they dive into shallow water. Dive only in the deep end of a pool and make sure that the water in lakes and at the beach is deep enough for diving. Also, be aware of any objects, such as large rocks, that may be hidden under the water.

6 Stay away from guns. There are at least 30,000 deaths and 100,000 injuries caused by guns each year in the United States.

7 Eat right. Your brain needs energy to work its best.

8 Dispose of chemicals properly. Many chemicals, such as pesticides and cleaners, contain neurotoxins that can kill or damage nerve cells. These dangerous chemicals can be found at home and in places of work.

Activities to Exercise Your Brain

CAFFEINE CONSUMPTION

You can call it 3,7-dihydro-1,3,7-trimethyl-1H-purine-2,6,-dione OR 1,3,7-trimethylxanthine, but what you are really talking about is caffeine. Caffeine, a central nervous system stimulant, may be the most popular drug in the world. We consume caffeine in coffee, tea, cocoa, chocolate, some soft drinks, and some drugs. The actual sources of caffeine are

continued on page 107

Table 5.1 **CAFFEINE CONTENT IN DRINKS AND FOODS**

Item	Item Size	Caffeine Content (mg)
Coffee	150 ml (5 oz)	60-150
Coffee, decaf	150 ml (5 oz)	2-5
Tea	150 ml (5 oz)	40-80
Hot cocoa	150 ml (5 oz)	1-8
Chocolate milk	225 ml	2-7
Jolt cola	12 oz	71
Josta	12 oz	58
Mountain Dew	12 oz	54
Surge	12 oz	51
Tab	12 oz	47
Diet Coke	12 oz	46
Coca-Cola Classic	12 oz	46
RC cola	12 oz	43
Dr. Pepper	12 oz	41
Mr. Pibb	12 oz	40
Pepsi cola	12 oz	38
7-Up	12 oz	0
Mug Root Beer	12 oz	0
Sprite	12 oz	0

Item	Item Size	Caffeine Content (mg)
Starbucks coffee ice cream	1 cup	40-60
Dannon coffee yogurt	8 oz	45
Chocolate bar	50 g	3-63
Chunky bar	1 bar (40 g)	11.6
100 Grand bar	1 bar (43 g)	11.2
Nestlé Crunch bar	1 bar (40 g)	10
Krackel bar	1 bar (47 g)	8.5
Peanut butter cup	1 pk (51 g)	5.6
Kit Kat bar	1 bar (46 g)	5
Mr. Goodbar	1 bar (50 g)	5
Raisinets	10 pieces (10 g)	2.5
Butterfinger bar	1 bar (61 g)	2.4
Baby Ruth bar	1 bar (60 g)	2.4
Special Dark sweet chocolate bar	1 bar (41 g)	31
Chocolate brownie	1.25 oz	8
Chocolate chip cookie	30 g	3-5
Chocolate ice cream	50 g	2-5
Milk chocolate	1 oz	1-15
Bittersweet chocolate	1 oz	5-35
After Eight mint	2 pc (8 g)	1.6
Jell-O Pudding Pop, chocolate	1 bar (77 g)	2

Sources: J.A.T. Pennington. *Food Values of Portions Commonly Used* (16th Edition). Philadelphia: J.B. Lippincott, 1994; Soft Drink Manufacturers Association; United States Department of Agriculture, Human Nutrition Information Service, Handbook #8-14 (1986) and Handbook #8-19 (1991); Starbucks Co. Information Pamphlet

coffee beans, tea leaves, kola nuts, and cacao pods. Pure caffeine is odorless and has a bitter taste.

How much caffeine do you consume each day? In a notebook, keep track of the products with caffeine that you consume. Write down the name of the product, the amount you consume of each product (for example, the number of ounces, grams, cups, bars, pills), the amount of caffeine in each product, and the time that you consumed the product. Use separate papers if you want to track your caffeine consumption on different days.

● ● ● ● ●

MR. EGGHEAD

Protect your brain! Your skull and cerebrospinal fluid help protect your brain from sudden impacts. "Mr. Egghead" will show you how this works. Mr. Egghead is a raw egg. The inside of the egg represents the brain and the eggshell represents the pia mater (the innermost layer of the meninges, the covering of the brain and spinal cord).

Put Mr. Egghead into a plastic container that is slightly larger than the egg. The container represents the skull. Put a tight top on the container and shake it. Shaking the container should damage the "brain" (a broken egg).

Repeat this experiment with a new Mr. Egghead, except this time fill the container with water. The water represents cerebrospinal fluid. Shaking the container should not cause the "brain damage" as before because the fluid cushions the brain from injury.

Drop the container with Mr. Egghead and check for damage
1 With fluid in the container
2 Without fluid in the container
3 With different fluids or materials (sand, rocks)
4 Using different shaped containers

Materials

◆ Eggs (at least two)
◆ Markers to draw on a face (waterproof)
◆ Plastic container with top
◆ Water (to fill the container)

Glossary

Action potential Electrical "all-or-none" impulse that transmits information within the nervous system.

Ambidextrous Able to use either hand to perform tasks such as writing and eating.

Amygdala Brain structure that is part of the limbic system; implicated in emotion.

Arachnoid Middle layer of the membranes that cover the brain and spinal cord (meninges).

Astrocyte (astroglia) Glial cell that supports neurons.

Autonomic nervous system Part of the nervous system that controls many organs and muscles within the body in an involuntary, reflexive manner.

Axon The part of the neuron that takes information away from the cell body.

Basal ganglia Areas of the brain that are important for controlling movement; includes the putamen, caudate nucleus, globus pallidus, subthalamic nucleus, and substantia nigra.

Basilar membrane Structure in the inner ear that contains hair cells.

Blood-brain barrier (BBB) A system of capillaries and glial cells in the brain that prevents specific substances from entering the brain.

Brain stem The central core of the brain that is responsible for basic life functions such as breathing and maintaining heart rate and blood pressure.

Broca's area Area in the frontal lobe of the brain that is important for speech production.

Central nervous system The brain and spinal cord.

Cerebellum Area of the brain that is important for balance and posture.

Cerebral aqueduct Part of the ventricular system that connects the third and fourth ventricles, also called the aqueduct of Sylvius.

Cerebral cortex Outermost layer (the gray matter) of the cerebral hemisphere.

Cerebrospinal fluid (CSF) Clear fluid in the ventricular system that functions to protect the brain, transport hormones, and remove waste products.

Cilia Small hairs.

Circadian rhythm Physiological processes, functions, or behaviors that are related to the 24-hour cycle of light and dark.

Cochlea Structure of the inner ear that is important for hearing.

Cone Cell in the retina that is important for color vision and detailed sight.

Cornea Transparent front coat of the eye.

Corpus callosum Large collection of axons that connect the left and right hemispheres of the brain.

Cranial nerves Twelve pairs of nerves that exit from the brain.

Dendrites Extensions on neurons that receive and deliver information to the cell body.

Dura mater Outermost layer of the membranes surrounding the brain and spinal cord (meninges).

Ectoderm Embryonic tissue from which the nervous system develops.

Electroencephalogram Record of electrical activity of the brain obtained from electrodes placed on the scalp.

Electroencephalograph Machine used to record the electrical activity of the brain.

Encephalization Process of brain formation during embryonic development.

Endoplasmic reticulum A network of membranes in a cell that is involved in the synthesis and transport of proteins.

Enteric nervous system Part of the autonomic nervous system consisting of a meshwork of nerves that innervate the gastrointestinal tract, pancreas, and gall bladder.

Fovea Central part of the retina; area of the retina with most accurate vision.

Glia Non-neural support cells of the nervous system.

Golgi apparatus Membrane-bound cell structure important in packaging peptides and proteins (including neurotransmitters) into vesicles.

Gray matter Areas of the nervous system with a high density of nerve cell bodies.

Gustation The sense of taste.

Gyrus (plural: gyri) Hill or bump on the surface of the brain.

Hemisphere One side of the cerebrum.

Hippocampus Area of the limbic system important for memory.

Hormone Chemical released into the bloodstream that controls functions of the body.

Hypothalamus Brain structure that monitors internal environment and attempts to maintain balance of these systems; also controls the pituitary gland.

Incus One of the three bones in the middle ear.

Iris Muscles of the eye that control the size of the pupil.

Lens Transparent structure in the eye that focuses light on the retina.

Limbic system Interconnected areas of the brain important for emotional and other behaviors.

Malleus One of the three bones in the middle ear.

Meninges Series of three membranes (dura mater, arachnoid, pia mater) that cover the brain and spinal cord.

Mitochondria Cellular structures that produce energy to fuel cellular activities.

Myelin Fatty substance that surrounds some axons.

Neuron Nerve cell.

Neurotransmitters Chemicals that transmit information across the synapse to communicate from one neuron to another.

Nodes of Ranvier Short segments of an axon that do not have a myelin coating.

Olfaction The sense of smell.

Olfactory epithelium Membrane that contains receptor cells for smell.

Parasympathetic nervous system Division of the autonomic nervous system that works to save energy.

Peripheral nervous system Network of nerves outside of the brain and spinal cord.

Photoreceptors Cells in the retina of the eye that are sensitive to light.

Pia mater Innermost layer of the membranes that surround the brain and spinal cord (meninges).

Pupil Hole in the center of the eye through which light passes.

Rapid eye movement (REM) sleep Stage of sleep during which a person's eyes move back and forth rapidly; most dreaming happens during REM sleep.

Receptors 1) Specialized cells that respond to different types of energy; 2) Areas on nerve cells that bind to neurotransmitters.

Reflex Automatic response to stimulation.

Retina Layer of tissue on the back portion of the eye that contains cells responsive to light (photoreceptors).

Ribosomes Cellular structure responsible for protein synthesis.

Rod Receptor in the retina important to vision in low light conditions.

Saltatory conduction Method of neurotransmission in a myelinated axon by which action potentials jump from node to node.

Soma The cell body of a neuron.

Somatic nervous system Peripheral nerves that send sensory information to the central nervous system and motor nerves that project to skeletal muscle.

Stapes One of three bones in the middle ear.

Sulcus (plural: sulci) Groove located on the surface of the brain.

Sympathetic nervous system Division of the autonomic nervous system that works in fight-or-flight situations.

Synapse Functional connection between a terminal of one neuron with a membrane of another neuron.

Synaptic terminal End of a neuron that contains vesicles of neurotransmitters.

Thalamus Brain structure important to sensory and motor functions.

Tympanic membrane Eardrum.

Umami One of the five basic tastes.

Ventricles Hollow channels in the brain that contain cerebrospinal fluid.

Vertebrae The bones that make up the spine.

Viscera Internal organs.

Vitreous humor Clear, jelly-like fluid found in the back portion of the eye that helps maintain the shape of the eye.

Wernicke's area Area of the cerebral cortex important for language comprehension.

White matter Areas of the nervous system with a high density of myelinated axons.

Bibliography

Bear, Mark F., Barry W. Connors, and Michael A. Paradiso. *Neuroscience: Exploring the Brain*. Baltimore: Williams & Wilkins, 2001.

Brynie, Faith Hickman. *101 Questions Your Brain Has Asked About Itself but Couldn't Answer...Until Now*. Brookfield, Conn.: The Millbrook Press, 1998.

Carlson, Neil R. *Physiology of Behavior (7th Edition)*. Boston: Allyn & Bacon, 2000.

Carter, Rita. *Mapping the Mind*. Berkeley: University of California Press, 1998.

Conlan, Roberta (editor). *States of Mind: New Discoveries About How Our Brains Make Us Who We Are*. New York: Dana Press, 1999.

Czerner, Thomas B. *What Makes You Tick? The Brain in Plain English*. New York: John Wiley and Sons, 2001.

Dement, William C., and Christopher Vaughan. *The Promise of Sleep: A Pioneer in Sleep Medicine Explains the Vital Connection Between Health, Happiness, and a Good Night's Sleep*. New York: Delacorte Press, 1999.

Drubach, Daniel. *The Brain Explained*. Upper Saddle River, N.J.: Prentice Hall, 2000.

Fleishman, John. *Phineas Gage: A Gruesome but True Story About Brain Science*. Boston: Houghton Mifflin Co., 2002.

Gazzaniga, Michael S. *The Cognitive Neurosciences*. Cambridge, Mass.: MIT Press, 2004.

Gazzaniga, Michael S., Richard B. Ivry, and G.R. Mangun. *Cognitive Neuroscience: The Biology of the Mind*. New York: Norton, 2002.

Greenfield, Susan A. *The Human Brain: A Guided Tour* (Science Masters series). New York: Basic Books, 1997.

Hyde, Margaret O., and John F. Setaro. *When the Brain Dies First.* Danbury, Conn.: Franklin Watts, 2000.

Kandel, Eric R., James H. Schwartz, and Thomas M. Jessell. *Principles of Neural Science, 4th edition.* New York: McGraw-Hill/Appleton & Lange, 2000.

Purves, Dale, George J. Augustine, David Fitzpatrick, William C. Hall, Anthony-Samuel Lamantia, James O. McNamara, and S. Mark Williams (editors). *Neuroscience.* Sunderland, Mass.: Sinauer Associates, Inc., 2004.

Ramachandran, V.S., and Sandra Blakeslee. *Phantoms in the Brain: Probing the Mysteries of the Human Mind.* New York: William Morrow & Company, 1998.

Ratey, John J. *A User's Guide to the Brain: Perception, Attention, and the Four Theaters of the Brain.* New York: Pantheon Books, 2001.

Society for Neuroscience. *Brain Facts.* Washington, D.C.: The Society for Neuroscience, 2002.

Stafford, Tom, and Matt Webb. *Mind Hacks: Tips & Tools for Using Your Brain.* Sebastopol, Calif.: O'Reilly Media, Inc., 2005.

Further Reading

Baines, Francesca. *Senses: How We Connect With The World.* Danbury, Conn.: Grolier Educational, 1998.

Ballard, Carol. *How Do We Think?* (How Your Body Works series). Austin, Tex.: Raintree Steck-Vaughn Publishers, 1998.

Barrett, Susan L. *It's All in Your Head: A Guide to Understanding Your Brain and Boosting Your Brain Power.* Minneapolis: Free Spirit Publishing, 1992.

Burrell, Brian. *Postcards From the Brain Museum: The Improbable Search for Meaning in the Matter of Famous Minds.* New York: Broadway Books, 2004.

Cleveland, Donald. *How Do We Know How the Brain Works.* New York: Rosen, 2005.

Conlan, Roberta (editor). *States of Mind: New Discoveries About How Our Brains Make Us Who We Are.* New York: Dana Press, 1999.

Cromwell, Sharon. *How Do I Know It's Yucky? And Other Questions About the Senses* (Body Wise series). New York: Heineman Library, 1998.

Cromwell, Sharon. *Why Do I Laugh or Cry? And Other Questions About the Nervous System* (Body Wise series). Des Plaines, Ill.: Rigby Interactive Library, 1998.

Ehrlich, Fred. *You Can't Use Your Brain If You're a Jellyfish.* Maplewood, N.J.: Blue Apple Books, 2005.

Firlik, Katrina. *Another Day in the Frontal Lobe: A Brain Surgeon Exposes Life on the Inside.* New York: Random House, 2006.

Fleischman, John. *Phineas Gage: A Gruesome but True Story About Brain Science.* Boston: Houghton Mifflin Co., 2002.

Goodman, Susan E. *Unseen Rainbows, Silent Songs: The World Beyond Your Senses*. New York: Atheneum Books for Young Readers, 1995.

Klemm, W.R. *Thank You, Brain, For All You Remember. What You Forgot Was My Fault*. Bryan, Tex.: Benecton Press, 2004.

Kramer, Stephen. *Hidden Worlds: Looking Through a Scientist's Microscope*. Boston: Houghton Mifflin Co., 2001.

Levert, Suzanne. *The Brain*. Tarrytown, N.Y.: Benchmark Books, 2002.

Parker, Steve and David West. *Brain Surgery for Beginners and Other Major Operations for Minors: A Scalpel-Free Guide to Your Insides*. New York: Scholastic, Inc., 1993.

Restak, Richard M. *The Secret Life of the Brain*. Washington, D.C.: Joseph Henry Press, 2001.

Rowan, Peter. *Big Head! A Book About Your Brain and Your Head*. New York, NY: Alfred A. Knopf, 1998.

Simon, Seymour. *The Brain: Our Nervous System*. New York: William Morrow, 1997.

Stafford, Tom and Matt Webb. *Mind Hacks: Tips and Tools for Using Your Brain*. Sebastopol, Calif.: O'Reilly, 2005.

Walker, Richard. *Brain: Our Body's Nerve Center*. Danbury, Conn.: Grolier Educational, 1998.

WEB SITES

Brain: The World Inside Your Head
http://www.pfizer.com/brain/index.html

BrainConnection.com
http://www.brainconnection.com

Brainmatters.org
http://www.thebrainmatters.org/index.cfm?key=1.1.1

Brains Rule!
http://www.brainsrule.com/

BrainScience on the Move
http://www2.neuroscience.umn.edu/brainscience/cool_stuff.htm

Comparative Mammalian Brain Collections
http://www.brainmuseum.org/

Digital Anatomist Project
http://www9.biostr.washington.edu/da.html

ePsych
http://epsych.msstate.edu/

Franklin Institute – The Human Brain
http://www.fi.edu/brain/index.html

Neuroscience for Kids
http://faculty.washington.edu/chudler/neurok.html

Neuroscience Laboratory and Classroom Activities
http://www.nabt.org/sup/publications/nlca/nlca.htm

Probe the Brain
http://www.pbs.org/wgbh/aso/tryit/brain/

Seeing, Hearing, and Smelling the World
http://www.hhmi.org/senses/

Sheep Brain Dissection Guide
http://academic.uofs.edu/department/psych/sheep/f1.html

Society for Neuroscience
http://www.sfn.org

The Brain From Top to Bottom!
http://www.thebrain.mcgill.ca/flash/index_d.html

Virtual Neurophysiology Lab
http://www.hhmi.org/biointeractive/vlabs/index.html

Picture Credits

All illustrations © Infobase Publishing;
Cover photo © 2006 Jupiter Images Corporation.

Index

About the Author

Eric H. Chudler, Ph.D., is a research neuroscientist who has investigated the brain mechanisms of pain and nociception since 1978. Dr. Chudler received his Ph.D. from the Department of Psychology at the University of Washington in Seattle. He has worked at the National Institutes of Health and directed a laboratory in the neurosurgery department at Massachusetts General Hospital. Between 1991 and 2006, Dr. Chudler was a faculty member in the Department of Anesthesiology at the University of Washington. He is currently a research associate professor in the University of Washington Department of Bioengineering and director of education and outreach at University of Washington Engineered Biomaterials. Dr. Chudler's research interests focus on how areas of the central nervous system (cerebral cortex and basal ganglia) process information related to pain. He has also worked with other neuroscientists and teachers to develop educational materials to help students learn about the brain.

Find out more about Dr. Chudler and the fascinating world of neuroscience by visiting his Web site, Neuroscience for Kids, at http://faculty.washington.edu/chudler/neurok.html.